Heroes of
Fighter Command

KENT

Rupert Matthews

COUNTRYSIDE BOOKS
NEWBURY BERKSHIRE

First published 2007
© Rupert Matthews 2007

COUNTRYSIDE BOOKS
3 Catherine Road
Newbury, Berkshire

To view our complete range of books,
please visit us at
www.countrysidebooks.co.uk

ISBN 978 1 84674 038 1

The cover picture shows
No 3 Squadron at Hawkinge
(South Eastern Newspapers Ltd.)

Designed by Peter Davies, Nautilus Design

Produced through MRM Associates Ltd., Reading
Typeset by CJWT Solutions, St Helens
Printed by Cambridge University Press

*All material for the manufacture of this book
was sourced from sustainable forests.*

CONTENTS

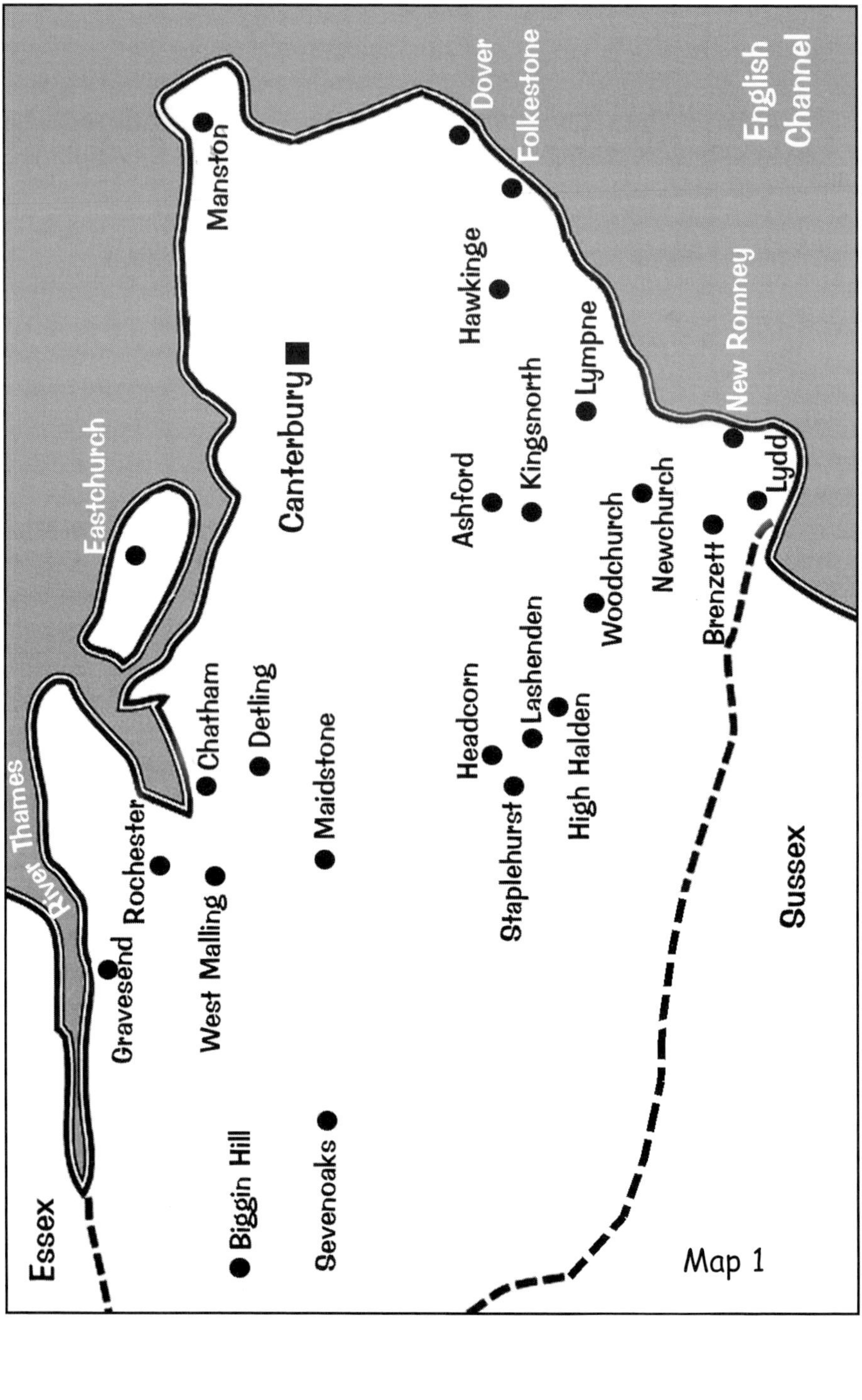

Essex
River Thames
Eastchurch
Manston
Dover
Folkestone
English Channel
Hawkinge
Lympne
New Romney
Canterbury
Ashford
Kingsnorth
Lydd
Woodchurch
Newchurch
Brenzett
Chatham
Detling
Maidstone
Headcorn
Lashenden
High Halden
Staplehurst
Sussex
Gravesend
Rochester
West Malling
Biggin Hill
Sevenoaks
Map 1

Preface

'Something which happened just before the war I shall never forget. I had a cousin aged about nineteen at that time. He had quite a few friends his own age and in those days it was considered the duty of older members of the family to take younger members out and about with them to give the parents a break. So when my cousin and his friends went – say playing tennis – my sister and I would be called for and taken with them to be ball boys and mind the jackets and wallets and so on while the tennis was played. At the end of the afternoon we were usually bought an ice cream for our efforts.

'Then one of the young men, Ron Ramsden his name was, somehow came into a little sum of money – left to him by an auntie or some such thing. He spent the money on buying himself a sports car. This was an unbelievable luxury in our working-class circles. I remember hearing my mother and my cousin's mother and aunties all gossiping together and saying how Ron should not have wasted the money on such a frivolous thing, but should have put it in the bank for his future because he would never get the chance to acquire such a nest egg again. It was quite a little scandal over the teacups.

'I remember one sunny day walking with my cousin towards his home where the family was going to meet for tea. We passed the home of Ron, who was outside in the road cleaning this sports car where it was standing at the curb. It was the only car parked in the entire road. He was so happy and proud, chatting to my cousin, and my cousin was looking admiringly at the smart car. Ron was blond and I can still see his yellow hair shining in the sun and blowing in the breeze. And I remember thinking he seemed so handsome and jolly and not at all wasteful and foolish as the aunties were saying.

'Three years later we were deep into the war. My cousin was in the army in Burma and the Battle of Britain was raging. My mother came home from visiting the aunties.

'"Ron Ramsden is dead," she said. "Killed flying with the RAF."

'By this time I was a young teenager and I remember thinking "Well I am glad he did buy that car. At least he had a little happiness before he died."'

So my mother told me of her childhood and about one friend who was snatched from her, fighting bravely in the skies over England. Ever since she told me of that dashing young man I have wanted to learn more about him and men like him. In researching this book I finally had the chance.

As the title of this book suggests, the main subjects are the men such as Ron Ramsden who fought in the RAF during the war, and particularly those who flew from Kent. For those readers with a wider interest in the RAF, who want to learn more about Fighter Command or Coastal Command as well as about the airfields and unit histories, I can do no better than advise you to purchase *Kent Airfields in the Second World War* by Robin J. Brooks, also published by Countryside Books, which makes a fine companion volume to this.

Of course, a book like this cannot possibly be the work of just one person. I would particularly like to thank Paul Lazell for permission to use photos taken by his father during his extensive career in the wartime RAF. Copies of these and other photos are available from Paul for a modest fee on paulsdadsphotos@aol.com. In this book his photos are indicated as (Paul Lazell). I must also thank Flt Lt Andrew Smith for his invaluable introductions to various RAF personnel, serving and retired. Shaun Smith, a retired RAF officer, has also helped out. I have made every effort to track down the copyright holders of material that I have used, but if I have missed anyone out please accept this as a genuine mistake and contact me so that matters can be put right in any future edition.

Kent is fortunate in having three magnificent museums devoted to the RAF. The RAF Manston Spitfire and Hurricane Memorial Trust has a museum just outside Kent International Airport (formerly RAF Manston) which houses a Spitfire and a Hurricane, plus a vast amount of other items and memorabilia. The Trust has been particularly helpful to me in producing this book and I would urge anyone interested in this subject to pay them a visit. In this book their photos are indicated as (Manston S&H Mem). The RAF Manston Museum nearby is also worth a visit. In this book their photos are indicated as (RAF Manston Mus). I would like to thank Brenzett Aeronautical Museum for their help and for permission to use photographs of their exhibits in this book. The museum stands in Ivychurch Road, just off the A2070, and is well worth a visit. Full details can be obtained on their website www.brenzettaero.co.uk. They have some particularly fine interactive exhibits for children of all ages. In this book their photos are indicated as (Brenzett AM).

Finally I must thank my wife for her patience and my daughter for her numerous interruptions.

Introduction

When war came, Kent was rapidly thrown into the maelstrom to become the most fought-over county in Britain. Dogfights took place daily on a massive scale, with hundreds of aircraft wheeling through the skies in deadly combat.

Yet only four years earlier, it had been a very different picture. Most of the RAF was abroad guarding colonial possessions against rebel tribesmen. The RAF in Britain, known as the Metropolitan Force, was dedicated to recruitment and training. There was no force dedicated to the defence of the realm.

Fighter Command was born in 1936 on the realisation that Adolf Hitler's Nazi Germany just might be an aggressive force that could be an enemy in some future war. Some, notably a backbench MP and former government minister named Winston Churchill, had been saying as much for years but it was not until an official government committee reached the same conclusion that anything much was done.

Even then the growth of the RAF was hampered by the fact that the Foreign Office persuaded the government to accept their estimates of Germany's armed strength over the estimates of the War Office. The fact that the Foreign Office figures were simply those announced by Hitler himself was not made clear at the time.

Perhaps because the Foreign Office figures indicated that Germany would not be ready to fight a war before 1942, that was the date set in RAF plans for when Britain would be ready too. The RAF was divided into five separate commands: Bomber Command, Coastal Command, Training Command, Maintenance Command and Fighter Command. Each command

Winston Churchill in September 1939 when he was in government as First Lord of the Admiralty. Before the war he had championed the cause of a much enlarged RAF, but had been largely ignored by the then government.

was headed by an Air Marshal, who was responsible to the Marshal of the Air Force and, through him, to the Air Ministry and so to the government.

The RAF was fortunate that the Air Marshal chosen as the first head of Fighter Command was Sir Hugh Dowding, widely known as 'Stuffy' due to his superficial manner akin to that of a retired old buffer. In fact Dowding had been a fighting pilot during the First World War and had gone on to command squadrons in various colonies before returning to Britain to take over RAF Research. He was thus both an expert combat pilot and well educated in the rapidly developing technology of aircraft and air weapons.

Dowding moved into Bentley Priory, an old manor house near Stanmore, and set to work making Fighter Command a reality. His task was to defend Britain against air attack of any kind. To do this he had just eighteen

Air Marshal Sir Hugh Dowding was head of Fighter Command when war broke out in 1939. He had been the commanding officer since 1936 and had moulded the air defences of the nation very much according to his own ideas.

squadrons equipped with biplane fighters. He also had command of the Observer Corps, a part-time civilian force whose job was to spot enemy aircraft and alert the RAF.

Dowding quickly established the principles of Fighter Command and the way it would defend Britain from enemy bombers. First the enemy had to be located and identified. Second the fighter squadrons had to find the enemy. Third the fighter pilots had to be able to shoot down the intruders. In 1936 Dowding's men were effectively unable to do any of these things.

When in charge of RAF Research, Dowding had allocated funds to the scientist Robert Watson-Watt who had come up with an idea that he called Radio Detection Finding, or RDF, but which would later become better known as radar. In 1936 Dowding summoned Watson-Watt to ask how the research was going. He was told that, as yet, the system could identify only large formations of aircraft and was quite unable to fix their numbers or heading with any accuracy, though their position could be found. Dowding ordered more research funds.

By the end of the year the world's first radar stations were being built in Kent. They were erected along the north coast and directed out over the North Sea so that they could pick up any formations of bombers heading from Germany to London. Watson-Watt promised that by 1942 he could have radar able to pinpoint even single aircraft with accuracy. Dowding told him to hurry up.

To plug the gaps until radar could be introduced properly, Dowding beefed up the Observer Corps. Thousands of men and women were recruited so that, when war came, there could be complete cover along the south and east coasts of Britain around the clock, despite the part-time nature of the volunteer commitment. They were given proper posts equipped with powerful binoculars, listening devices and sandbagged

One of the listening posts that dotted the coast of Kent in 1939. Before the development of radar the detection of approaching enemy bombers rested on these unlikely looking contraptions. By 1940 most of the south-east coast was covered by radar, but elsewhere amplified listening remained standard.

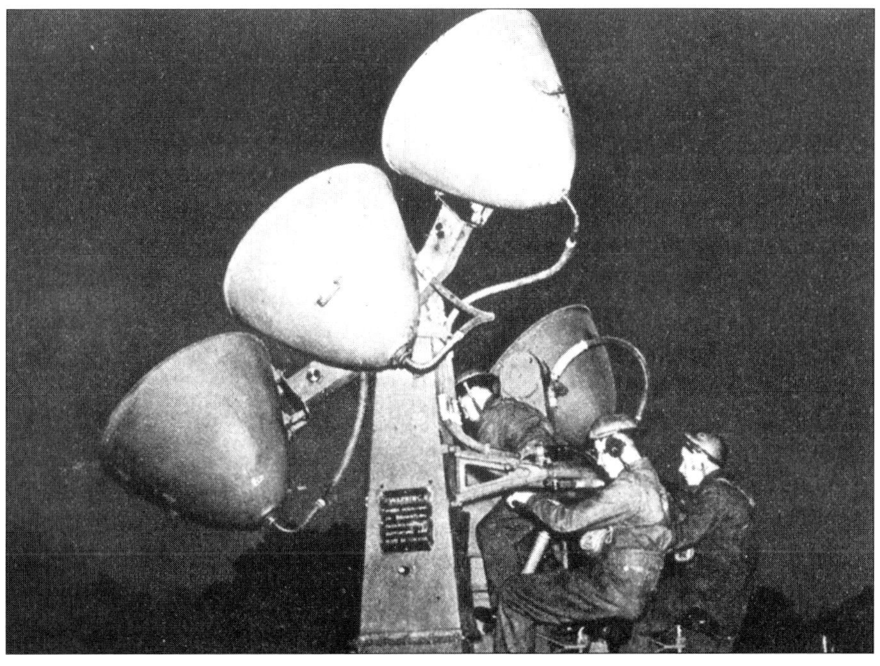

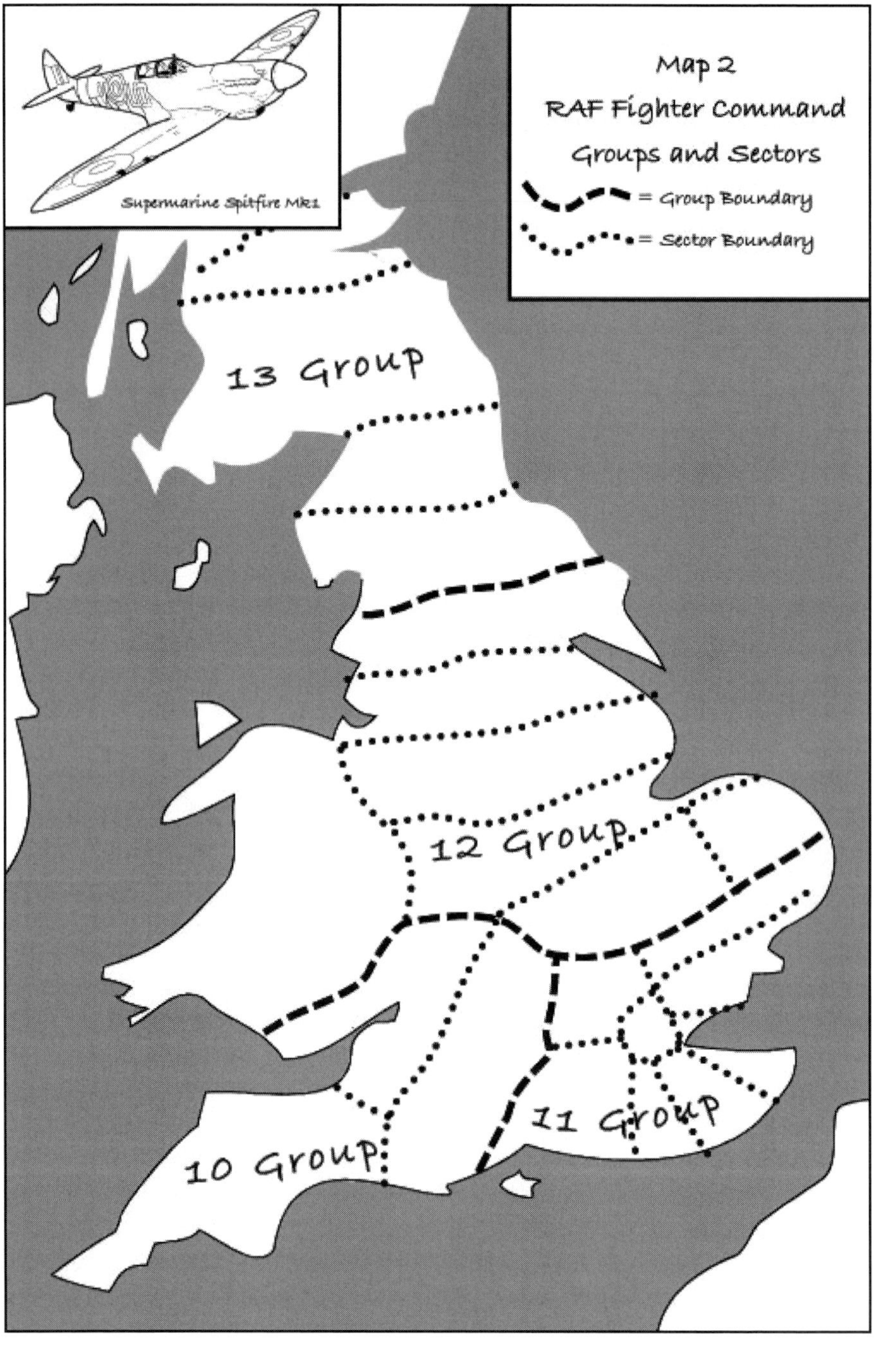

Supermarine Spitfire Mk1
Map 2
RAF Fighter Command
Groups and Sectors
= Group Boundary
= Sector Boundary
13 Group
12 Group
11 Group
10 Group

trenches, in which the observers could take cover if they were attacked.

In the event, the radar chain around Britain was substantially complete by the time war broke out in 1939. The Observer Corps remained in place to give visual confirmation of radar plots, and to cover those inland areas where the radar stations could not get a secure fix.

Dowding next divided the country up into groups. Kent came under 11 Group, which also covered Sussex, London and Essex. The south-west came under 10 Group, the midlands under 12 group and Scotland and northern England under 13 Group. Each group had its own commander, an air vice marshal, and was responsible for the administration of the squadrons within its area. At first only 11 Group and 12 Group were operational, the others being established when aircraft and pilots became available.

When it came to war, reports from radar and the Observer Corps would be sent simultaneously to Bentley Priory and to their local group HQ. It was up to the group commander to decide which squadrons to send up to combat any threat in his area. Dowding at Bentley Priory gave himself the task of keeping an eye on the national situation and ordering any co-operation between groups that might become necessary.

That left Dowding's third task: giving his fighter pilots the means to shoot down the enemy. When he took over in 1936 he found that Fighter Command had only biplane fighters, equipped with twin machine guns – not much different from those he had himself flown over France in 1917. Fortunately a range of new, improved fighters was in the pipeline and again Dowding was already familiar with them from his time in charge of research.

The first of the new aircraft to reach Fighter Command in December 1937 was the Hurricane, produced by the Hawker company. This single-engined monoplane packed a mighty punch with no fewer than eight machine guns in its wings. It could reach 324 mph and had a range of almost 600 miles, making it both faster than the biplanes it replaced and able to patrol for much longer. It was of relatively conventional construction, most of the fuselage being of fabric, painted with dope to keep it strong and airtight, which made it both cheap to make and easy to repair.

Six months later the Supermarine Spitfire reached Fighter Command. This magnificent aircraft could top 350 mph and had a range of over 500 miles, while still carrying the same eight-gun armament as the Hurricane.

A squadron of Hurricanes in 1939. The 12 aircraft are arranged in four groups of three aircraft, each group flying in a V-shaped formation. This is the notorious Vic formation, that was revealed to be so flawed when combat against the Luftwaffe began.

It could climb faster and fly faster than the Hurricane. The Spitfire was, moreover, a much more sophisticated aircraft with a stressed metal frame and delicate controls. This made it an expensive aircraft to build and one that was more difficult to repair in combat situations.

While the Hurricane and Spitfire were developed to be the main anti-bomber fighters for home defence, Fighter Command had other duties. One of the most crucial was to escort British bombers on their raids into Germany and to fend off German fighters. This task needed an aircraft that had a greater range than either the Spitfire or Hurricane, which meant the ability to carry much more fuel. This, in turn, made the aircraft heavier; so two engines were needed to get it off the ground. Yet the aircraft had to be nimble enough to behave as a fighter.

Dowding found his answer in the Blenheim, made by the Bristol Aircraft Company. The Blenheim was, in fact, merely a version of Bristol's 142 Transport aircraft, but with uprated engines, four forward-firing machine guns and a single machine gun in a dorsal turret. It could reach 278 mph and had a range of well over 1,000 miles.

A fourth modern fighter that would enter service in December 1939, after war had broken out, was the Defiant, manufactured by Boulton Paul. This aircraft could top 300 mph and had a range of 465 miles. Its unique feature was a turret carrying four machine guns, manned by a gunner, immediately behind the pilot. These guns were heavy weapons that were astonishingly accurate over long distances in the air. The idea was that the Defiant could break up enemy formations from a distance, allowing the nimbler Hurricanes and Spitfires to get in among the scattered bombers.

By the time war broke out in 1939, Dowding had made massive and wide-ranging improvements to Fighter Command. He had new aircraft, new organisation and new equipment. What he did not have was more time.

Hawker Hurricane

Type:	Single seat fighter
Engine:	1030 hp Rolls Royce Merlin
Wingspan:	40 ft
Length:	31 ft 5 in
Height:	13 ft
Weight:	Empty 4982 lb
	Loaded 6532 lb
Armament:	8 x 0.303 machine guns in wings
Max speed:	324 mph
Ceiling:	34,200 ft
Range:	600 miles
Production:	14,449

The first of the low-wing monoplane fighters to enter service with the RAF, the Hurricane was a vast improvement on any other aircraft then in British service. When war came it quickly proved itself to be a reliable fighter in combat conditions. It was beloved by its pilots as a 'steady gun platform' and was frequently employed to tackle German bombers, while the more agile Spitfires dealt with the fighters. The figures given above relate to the Hurricane MkI, the version that fought through the Battle of Britain. By 1941 the MkII was entering service with an uprated 1460 hp Merlin engine and consequent improvements in performance. The MkII could carry a range of weaponry, including twelve machine guns or four 20 mm cannons. The MkIIC could carry either 1000 lb of bombs or racks of rockets, and was known informally as the 'Hurribomber'. The Hurricane was still in service when the war ended in 1945.

Chapter 1

The Warbirds

In April 1939, just as the squadrons based in Kent were getting themselves sorted out and fitted in to Dowding's plan for Fighter Command, politics intruded in an unwelcome way. As war with Germany loomed closer, the French and British governments began detailed discussions on joint strategy. The French had to make the deeply embarrassing admission that their air force was simply not up to the task of facing the Luftwaffe.

The main French weakness was its fighters. The magnificent Dewoitine 520 was behind schedule, with only 30 of a planned 400 having been delivered, while the Potez 63 and Breguet 690 were outclassed by the German aircraft. The British government agreed to send four RAF squadrons equipped with Hurricanes to France if war broke out. Dowding was horrified, as this represented some 20 per cent of his squadrons with modern fighters. He was even less impressed when he got reports on the dire condition of the French airfields from which the squadrons were supposed to operate. Dowding earmarked some squadrons – none of them from Kent – for service in France but made it clear that he would not send them unless the airfields were improved.

Fighter Command in Kent suffered its first casualties even before war began. In early August 1939 a practice blackout was held across London. Two Hurricane pilots of 60a Squadron, Flying Officers Olding and Wollaston, were sent up to observe the results from the air. A gale blew

A squadron of Hurricane pilots race for their machines 'somewhere in France'.
The exercise was staged for the benefit of press photographers in October 1939
to show the readiness of RAF units in France.

up, and both men crashed into Tatsfield Hill when trying to land back at Biggin Hill. A few days later Winston Churchill dropped by to the officers' mess from his home nearby at Chartwell.

When war came, Kent had operational airfields at Biggin Hill, Gravesend, Manston, Lympne and Hawkinge, while West Malling was under construction. Of these, Biggin Hill was by far the most important. It had three operational squadrons: 32 and 79, flying Hurricanes, and 601, flying Blenheims. It was also the sector station, meaning that the various administration staff for Fighter Command in Kent were based here, as was the operations room, which kept in radio contact with the squadrons in the air and directed the aerial operations. It was the largest of all the bases with hangars, storerooms, repair workshops, offices, numerous barracks and a power station.

Gravesend was a civilian airfield, but it was requisitioned as soon as war seemed imminent. No squadrons were based here at first, the airfield operating as a satellite base to Biggin Hill. Manston fulfilled a similar function, while Lympne was a training base, as was Hawkinge. Hawkinge did, however, have 25 Squadron in residence, flying Blenheims.

In 1936 Manston had achieved a brief notoriety when it was the focus of Britain's only inter-war spy trial. A German doctor named Hermann Goertz was caught making detailed sketches of the airfield and found to have had regular contact with a young woman named Marianne Emig, who had meanwhile fled back to Germany and was thought to be linked to the SS. The Old Bailey jury found Goertz guilty of minor crimes, there not being enough evidence to prove him guilty of actual espionage. He was imprisoned for a few months, then deported. In 1942 he was arrested in Eire, where he was finally unmasked as a full-time SS agent.

Air Vice Marshal E.L. Gossage was in command of 11 Group, which included Kent, when war broke out. He and Dowding drew up their plans based on their estimates of the likely course of the war. They knew that any war would be triggered by German aggression in eastern Europe and believed that for the first few weeks at least the Luftwaffe would be chiefly concerned with events there. Any air attacks on Britain would, they thought, be nuisance raids or reconnaissance flights designed to test defences rather than inflict any serious damage.

Once Germany had crushed resistance in the east, Dowding reasoned, it would turn west. It was expected that German armies would invade France, probably marching through Belgium as they had done in 1914. Dowding expected that the Luftwaffe's lighter bombers and fighters would co-operate with the army in this attack, while the larger bombers would be sent to attack targets in Britain. It was expected that the German attack would be halted somewhere in Belgium or northern France, again as in 1914. At this point the war would either become a long, drawn-out attritional slogging match like the First World War, or the diplomats would patch up a compromise peace.

The key point for Dowding and Gossage was precisely where the German advance would be halted. Flying from known Luftwaffe bases in Germany, attacking bombers could reach London with ease, but cities such as Leicester and Newcastle were at the limits of their operational range, while Bristol and Liverpool were out of range completely. If, however, the Germans captured all of Belgium before being stopped, that would bring Plymouth and Cardiff into comfortable range of Hitler's bombers, while all the UK except Northern Ireland and the north of Scotland could be reached at extreme range.

A group of RAF pilots meet with their squadron intelligence officer after a mission in 1939 to discuss their observations and experiences. The wall behind is plastered with information on enemy bombers.

Dowding and Gossage knew that during the first phase the German aircraft would approach from due east over the North Sea. Even if all Belgium fell they would still be coming from the east, though they would have more time over Britain to find their targets, attack them and fend off fighters.

Dowding estimated that once war was declared he would have a period of time, ranging from a few weeks to a few months, of relative calm before any major German bombing attacks were made on Britain. In this he was at variance with the general public and the politicians, most of whom expected immediate and devastating bombing raids on London and other major cities.

As expected, war broke out with a German invasion of Poland. As Dowding had thought, the Luftwaffe was at first chiefly engaged in Poland. What neither Dowding nor any other senior military figures had foreseen was the speed of the German conquest of Poland. Although the Poles lacked tanks, they had a large and well-regarded army and an effective air force. With Poland gone by the end of September 1939, Dowding and his men braced themselves for the expected German onslaught.

A Bofors gun crew prepare for action during an exercise in 1939. These lightweight, mobile anti-aircraft guns formed the main defences around RAF Fighter Command bases during 1939 and 1940.

What nobody expected was the long period of quiet that was to earn itself the sobriquet 'Phoney War'. The term is somewhat misleading, as it refers only to the lack of action on the ground. In the air and at sea the war would be fought in deadly earnest.

In fact the first test for the men of Fighter Command in Kent had come just fifteen minutes after war was declared on 3 September. An unidentified aircraft was spotted on radar approaching the Kent coast. Bentley Priory and No.11 Group HQ were alerted and Biggin Hill ordered to send up fighters to intercept the intruder. Three Hurricanes of 32 Squadron were in the air and heading for Gravesend before the aircraft was identified as a French machine and the alert was cancelled.

Another alert came that evening when a listening post reported hearing the engines of aircraft approaching from the east. That alert was also cancelled, when it was realised that the listening device was picking up the noise of a fridge motor in the next room.

On 16 October a German bombing raid was launched against British warships in the Firth of Forth. The local fighters were sent up, and shot down one bomber for no loss. Still Fighter Command in Kent saw no real action, though they were sent up on daily patrols and frequently went after supposed intruders, which turned out to be French or neutral aircraft, or even flocks of starlings.

Kent's squadrons first saw action on 21 November. Flying Officer James Davies and Sergeant Brown of 79 Squadron out of Biggin Hill were on a routine patrol over Folkestone in poor weather when they received a radio message telling them that radar had picked up an unidentified aircraft out to sea. The two pilots turned their Hurricanes in the designated direction and within minutes spotted a Dornier 17 at 15,000 ft, apparently on a reconnaissance mission.

At 21,000 ft, the Hurricanes had a clear height advantage. Davies attacked first, opening fire when 600 ft from the target. Brown then joined the attack, watching as the German flipped on its back and dived into cloud. Not wanting to think the German had been only damaged and could limp home, Brown dived into the cloud, emerging from its underside to see the Dornier crash into the sea trailing smoke. It was the first German aircraft shot down by the men of Fighter Command in Kent.

A week later, on 29 November, 25 Squadron at Hawkinge and 601 Squadron at Biggin Hill between them sent up 12 Blenheims. Their target was the German seaplane base at Borkum. The seaplanes had been coming

A Dornier Do18 flyingboat brought down into the sea during April 1940 by fighters flying out of Kent. The Do18 was a long-range naval reconnaissance aircraft.

out night after night to lay mines along the British coast. Their high speed and low flying made them almost impossible to catch, so now Fighter Command was trying to catch them in their lair just before they took off.

As dusk began to gather over Borkum, the Blenheims roared in from the sea. Flying one aircraft was Flight Lieutenant Max Aitken, son of the newspaper magnate Lord Beaverbrook. The twin-engined fighters came in at under 100 ft, concentrating their fire on the seaplanes, but also blazing away at anything they saw. The raid lasted less than ten minutes. Five seaplanes were destroyed, a patrol boat sunk and a supply ship in the harbour damaged. All the aircraft got back safely. 'The Germans probably never thought that they would have to hit anything flying so low,' commented one pilot on his return.

Early in November Manston shed its training personnel, who moved to Blackpool, while Manston became a fully operational fighter station. An aircraft flying from the airfield at the end of the month went missing and nobody ever learned the fate of the pilot.

The airfield at Hawkinge experienced a rather more eventful Phoney

A pre-war photo of Hurricane fighters flying in formation. The Mk1 Hurricane, shown here, was armed with eight 0.303 machine guns and was much praised for being a stable gun platform in a dogfight.

War than some, though not much of it involved actual combat. No.3 Squadron flew its Hurricanes in to take up residence in December, a landing that was made memorable by the fact that they could not find the airfield at first because the pilots had not been told that it had been camouflaged the day before their arrival. Various Army Co-operation squadrons arrived, then left as they made their way to France. In January the highly secretive No.1 Pilotless Aircraft Unit arrived. Its job was to fly a collection of radio-controlled obsolete aircraft around to mislead the Germans as to how many aircraft were stationed in Kent. An equally secretive autogyro test unit also arrived, but it was in February that the most important unit arrived. This was a group of German-speaking WAAFs, who worked shifts in a hut on the edge of the airfield to provide a 24-hour listening service to record German radio broadcasts. In March, 416 Squadron was formed at Hawkinge, but without either aircraft or men. It was disbanded three weeks later, then re-formed and left.

Through all this the only casualty was Sergeant Lomay, whose Hurricane crashed due to unknown factors when coming in to land after a patrol.

By February the squadrons of Fighter Command in Kent had settled down to a steady routine. Aircraft were scrambled to meet incoming raids, that turned out to be either a lone German aircraft that had already fled, or a false alarm – known as X-raids. The only real duties involved escorting convoys of ships along the coast to protect them against German bombers that never came.

One change that did affect the men and women serving in Kent came in February 1940, when Gossage was moved to become Inspector General of the RAF – an administrative post linked to keeping the RAF equipped with modern aircraft in sufficient numbers. His place in charge of 11 Group was taken by Air Vice Marshal Keith Park. Park came direct from Bentley Priory, where he had been acting as Dowding's second in command. He knew Dowding's methods and got on well with him. In the desperate weeks to come the two men would co-operate easily.

By April the bitter weather of the coldest winter in 40 years came to an end. Hitler launched his unexpected assaults on Denmark and Norway. Denmark surrendered almost at once, and although the more remote areas of Norway held out for some months the bulk of that country was quickly under the German heel. It was clear that it would not be long before Britain and France felt the might of the German armed forces.

Air Vice Marshal Keith Park wearing his famous white flying helmet in the cockpit of his personal Spitfire, in which he visited airfields throughout his 11 Group Command in 1940. (Manston S&H Mem)

Gloster Gladiator

Type: Single seat fighter
Engine: 840 hp Bristol Mercury
Wingspan: 32 ft 3 in
Length: 27 ft 5 in
Height: 10 ft 4 in
Weight: Empty 3450 lb
Loaded 4750 lb
Armament: 4 x 0.303 machine guns in nose and under wings
Max speed: 253 mph
Ceiling: 33,000 ft
Range: 428 miles
Production: 768

The Gloster Gladiator was the last biplane to enter service with the RAF, first reaching squadrons in February 1937. Despite its outdated appearance the Gladiator was in many ways a most advanced aircraft. It had a fully enclosed cockpit, a metal propeller and a relatively heavy armament. By the time war broke out Fighter Command had removed the Gladiator from front line service, although it was retained for local use – six of the Gladiators were stationed to protect Plymouth docks, for instance. In 1940 three Gladiators – nicknamed *Faith*, *Hope* and *Charity* – guarded Malta against the massed raids of the Italian air force. By 1942 the Gladiator had left combat duties, being relegated to gathering meteorological data.

Chapter 2

Dunkirk

In late April and early May 1940 the men flying with the squadrons of Fighter Command that had been sent to France noticed a distinct change in the war. While most others had their eyes on Norway and still talked about the Phoney War, the men of Fighter Command in France found themselves up against increasing numbers of Luftwaffe intruders. Most German aircraft were scouts, rather than bombers, but it was obvious to those with eyes to see that some major operation was in the offing.

The storm broke just before dawn on 10 May when the German panzers surged over the borders of France, Belgium and Holland. Even before the Fighter Command squadrons in France were alerted to the invasion, their airbases were shaken by bomb blasts as German bombers screamed in to wreak destruction and gain control of the air. Many of the aircraft were destroyed on the ground that morning.

To try to make up for the unfolding carnage, 600 Squadron was ordered off from Biggin Hill to attack Rotterdam airport, where large numbers of German airborne troops were landing. The six Blenheims flew low all the way, and launched their attack from rooftop height. The damage they inflicted was impressive, but unknown to them a large force of Messerschmitt 110s was circling above. Down came the 110s and in less than two minutes five of the six British aircraft were smoking wrecks.

The lone survivor was piloted by Flying Officer Norman Hayes with air gunner Corporal George Holmes. The first spray of bullets from the Germans ruptured a fuel line, spraying fuel around the interior of the aircraft. While Holmes fired back at the pursuers he calmly gave

A group of No.32 Squadron pilots photographed at Biggin Hill in 1940.

instructions to Hayes on evasive manoeuvres to avoid the incoming fire. After several tense moments the 110s gave up the chase, allowing the Blenheim to head for home.

As they tore at low altitude across the Dutch landscape, Hayes spotted a German Junkers Ju52 transport aircraft ahead and above them. Despite the damage to their own aircraft, the British pair attacked, sending the enemy down with one engine on fire. Only after this did they take their damaged aircraft home to Biggin Hill.

Dowding was ordered to send three squadrons of fighters to France to make up for the early losses. He protested, but political pressure from the French forced British Prime Minister Churchill to insist. Dowding wriggled by sending over the required number of fighters, but keeping the squadrons' headquarters and base personnel in England.

On 15 May Dowding attended a meeting of the War Cabinet, chaired by Churchill. On the table was another request from the French for air support in the form of squadrons from RAF Fighter Command to be sent to northern France. Dowding objected to the idea. He then got up from

Recovering crew work on a Spitfire that returned damaged to Hawkinge in the spring of 1940 and ended up in a hedge after its brakes failed.

his seat and walked to Churchill to whom he handed a graph showing the loss of RAF fighters plotted against time and with the flow of replacements clearly marked. Churchill stared at the graph for a few moments in silence. Then he ordered that no more aircraft should go to France. What Dowding had demonstrated was that not only would the French Air Force be wiped out within a fortnight, but so would any RAF fighters sent to France. If more RAF fighters went to France, Britain would be without any fighter cover should Hitler decide to invade. And without air cover the Navy was unlikely to be able to defend the Channel.

The next day, Dowding sat down and wrote his famous 'minimum fighter strength' letter to the Air Minister to put on the official record his comments at the cabinet meeting. It read, in part:

'Sir,

I have the honour to refer to the very serious calls which have recently been made upon the Home Defence Fighter Units in an attempt to stem the German invasion on the Continent. I presume that there is no one who will deny that England should fight on, even though the remainder of Europe is dominated by the Germans. For this purpose it is necessary to retain some minimum fighter strength in this country. I would remind the Air Council that the last estimate which they made as to the force necessary to defend this country was 52 squadrons, and my strength has now been reduced to 36 squadrons. It should be made clear to the Allied Commanders on the Continent that not a single aeroplane from Fighter Command will be sent across the Channel, no matter how desperate the situation may become.

'I believe that, if an adequate Fighter force is kept in this country, if the fleet remains in being and if Home Forces are suitably organised to resist invasion we should be able to carry on the war single-handed for some time, if not indefinitely. But if the Home Defence Force (of the RAF) is drained away in desperate attempts to remedy the situation in France, defeat in France will involve the final complete and irremediable defeat of this country.

'I have the honour to be, Sir, Your obedient servant

HCT Dowding.'

Even as Dowding wrote, the panzers were sweeping through northern France on their way to the English Channel. About twenty per cent of Fighter Command's strength had already been lost and the French Air Force was on its way to destruction – and there was no sign that the Luftwaffe had exerted itself overmuch. The speed and direction of the German advance caught everyone by surprise. The British, French and Belgian armies were tumbled back in confusion – those of the Netherlands had been overwhelmed in the first days of fighting. Several RAF squadrons had to evacuate almost as the panzers arrived at the gates, abandoning fuel, equipment and aircraft in their haste to get away.

Cut off from the main French armies to the south and pummelled by Luftwaffe bombing, Lord Gort ordered the British armies in France and Belgium to retreat to the coast in the hope that the Royal Navy could take them home. So quickly had the panzers advanced that there was only one port left in Allied hands: Dunkirk.

Dowding was ordered to send his fighters to provide air cover to the naval evacuation, code-named Dynamo. The need was urgent and hundreds of thousands of lives were at risk. The fighters flying out of Kent

General Lord Gort VC. In 1939 he was appointed to command the British Forces in France. It was Gort's decision to ignore the protests of his French colleagues and retreat to Dunkirk that allowed the British army to escape annihilation in 1940.

would have to cross 60 miles of open sea to reach Dunkirk, where they would be out of range of both their radar support and the radio signals from base. The Luftwaffe, by contrast, was now flying out of captured French airfields barely five miles from Dunkirk.

Outnumbered and at a serious distance disadvantage they might have been, but the men of Fighter Command in Kent knew that they had to go; so go they did. Many found themselves taking off at dawn, fighting over Dunkirk, then returning to refuel, only to be sent up again without a pause. Some pilots went over four times each day while the evacuation proceeded.

To meet the urgent need for fighters over Dunkirk several squadrons from elsewhere were moved into Kent. Among these was 264 Squadron from Duxford, which moved its Defiants temporarily to Manston on 23 May. They flew their first patrol to Dunkirk that afternoon and remained in almost constant combat throughout the evacuation. On 24 May the Defiants shot down a Messerschmitt 110 that strayed too close, and the next day flew two squadron-strength patrols to Dunkirk. On the 26th they were escorting a convoy but on 27 May returned to the skies over Dunkirk. For the first time in the war the Defiants found a squadron of Heinkel 111 bombers. They shot down three Heinkels for no loss, forcing the rest of the Germans to abandon their mission. It seemed that the Defiants could fulfil the designed role of turret fighters, namely to break up enemy formations from the comparative safety of the beam.

On 26 May Pilot Officer William McKnight of 242 Squadron, flying temporarily from Biggin Hill rather than the unit's base at Coltishall, was with his squadron when they attacked a force of German bombers heading for Dunkirk. McKnight shot down one German aircraft and damaged another before turning on a third. This enemy turned away and dived at high speed for the east. Undeterred McKnight likewise dived for speed. The chase went on for more than 20 miles before the Hurricane closed with the German and McKnight was able to blast it from the skies.

Pulling up, McKnight realised that he was over enemy territory and had only a vague idea of where he was. He decided to head north-west in the hope of finding the coast and to keep at low level to escape the notice of enemy fighters. As he tore across the landscape, McKnight noticed a railway train pulling a long line of flatbed trucks loaded with artillery. Knowing they could only be German guns, McKnight altered course to fly

The pilots of 74 Squadron photographed in Kent in May 1940. Of the men shown here a total of nine would be killed in action, five of them during the Battle of Britain. (Manston S&H Mem)

along the train, his machine guns chattering. How much damage he did is unknown, but his last view over his shoulder as he streaked for home was of smoke pouring from the train.

On 28 May No.213 Squadron, in Hurricanes, were heading for Dunkirk when they spotted a formation of about 50 German bombers. The Hurricanes dived to the attack, but were at once set upon by 30 escorting German Messerschmitt Bf 109 fighters. Sergeant Samuel Butterfield turned his Hurricane to face the oncoming Germans and opened fire. A 109 promptly exploded in a ball of flame, but Butterfield had no time to savour his triumph as a second German came at him. Firing again, Butterfield saw this second German peel away with smoke pouring from its engine. Clear of the fighters, Butterfield now turned on the bombers. He saw a Junkers 88 making a diving attack and plunged after it, coming up on its quarter. The German crew seemed intent on their target below, for they did not see Butterfield until he opened fire. Pieces flew off the German aircraft, which then flipped on to its back and crashed into the sea.

This time it was Butterfield who was too busy watching his target. He did not see a Messerschmitt Bf 110 coming up behind him until a cannon shell slammed into his cockpit, causing the instrument panel to explode in a shower of fragments. Butterfield hauled his aircraft round in a tight turn, carefully exploiting the chief weakness in combat of the 110, and fired his remaining bullets into the German, which broke away and dived out of control.

Now out of ammunition, short of fuel and with no working instruments, Butterfield turned his damaged aircraft for home. As he was limping alone over the sea a second 110 came into view. Butterfield threw his Hurricane into a series of desperate turns and flips to escape the attack, but in vain. Two more cannon shells hit his aircraft, tearing the fuselage and severing control cables. A third shell then hit the engine, setting it on fire.

As flames engulfed the aircraft, Butterfield threw open his cockpit and leapt clear into the blue sky. His parachute opened and as he floated down Butterfield saw the 110 circle, then head off back towards Dunkirk. Butterfield splashed heavily into the sea, inflated his lifejacket and discarded the parachute.

Alone with the wind and the waves, Butterfield was glad to find that he was not injured, but rather alarmed to find that neither aircraft nor ships were in sight. It was with some surprise that an hour or so later Butterfield saw a civilian yacht crowded with soldiers hove into sight. It was the first time that he had realised the Navy had drafted in the now famous 'small boats of Dunkirk' to help with the evacuation. That evening Butterfield was put ashore at Dover and the next day he was back with his squadron. He was awarded an immediate Distinguished Flying Medal (DFM) for his exploits.

Also shot down that day was Pilot Officer Douglas Grice of 32 Squadron. His parachute landed him inside the defensive perimeter of Dunkirk. Fortunately unwounded, Grice walked down to the beaches and, after a gruelling wait of a couple of days, got on a destroyer and returned to England. His comrades were delighted to see him turn up, as they feared he had been killed.

Another pilot of 32 Squadron shot down over Dunkirk was Flying Officer 'Millie' Milner. He failed to return, but a few weeks later the squadron got a postcard sent from a German prisoner of war camp. It read 'Sorry I left you the other day. I wasn't thinking. Wonder if you are still at The Bump. Do drop in and see me any time you are around these parts. Love to everyone and good luck. Millie'.

The high rate of loss meant that new pilots were desperately needed. The

The beach at Dunkirk photographed from a Royal Navy ship waiting offshore to pick up a load of British soldiers. Fighter Command flew hundreds of sorties to Dunkirk to try to keep the Luftwaffe away from the beaches.

day after Butterfield's close escape Sergeant Ken Townsend joined 79 Squadron at Biggin Hill from a training unit. That very afternoon he was sent up on his first combat mission over Dunkirk. His flight commander gave Townsend the traditional pre-combat talk about the dangers of flying straight, the need to keep an eye on the sun for enemy aircraft and ended with the usual 'stick to me like glue'. Both men were equally surprised when within seconds of encountering a squadron of 109s Townsend shot one down. Next day he shot down a second German aircraft in the morning and a third in the afternoon. It was Fighter Command's fastest 'hat-trick' of the war.

That same day, 29 May, the Defiants of 264 Squadron were back in action, still flying from their temporary forward base at Manston. Squadron Leader Hunter led twelve of the peculiar turret fighters to Dunkirk. They were accompanied by two squadrons of Hurricanes flying at higher altitude. The intention was for the Defiants to break up the enemy formations so that the Hurricanes could then close in for the kill. Things did not quite work out like that.

Over the Channel the Hurricanes were attacked by a force of 110s. With the Hurricanes busy, six 109s dived out of the sun to attack the Defiants. The British gunners let fly with their heavy machine guns and within seconds four of the Germans had been shot from the sky. One Defiant turned for home badly damaged and with a dead gunner, but the others pushed on towards Dunkirk. A Junkers 87, the famous Stuka divebomber, wandered within range and was shot down, apparently without its crew having noticed the British planes.

Over Dunkirk the Defiants were bounced by a squadron of 110s and another of 109s. Hunter ordered his aircraft to adopt the conventional spiralling dive formation in which each Defiant was covered by the guns of another. Seven 110s were shot down, as were three 109s. Combat over, the pilots of 264 headed for Manston.

That afternoon they were sent back to Dunkirk, again with Hurricanes above them. This time they arrived without incident just as a mass of Stukas went down to divebomb the British soldiers on the beaches. The Defiants swooped down to low level to catch the Germans as they pulled out of their dives, when they would be most vulnerable. The tactic worked superbly and soon eighteen Stukas were clawed out of the skies. Turning for home, the Defiants met a force of Junker 88s coming the other way, and shot one down.

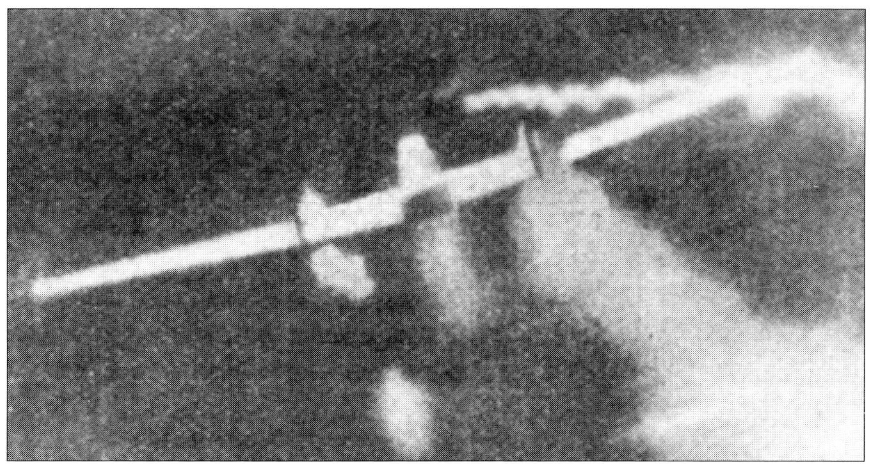

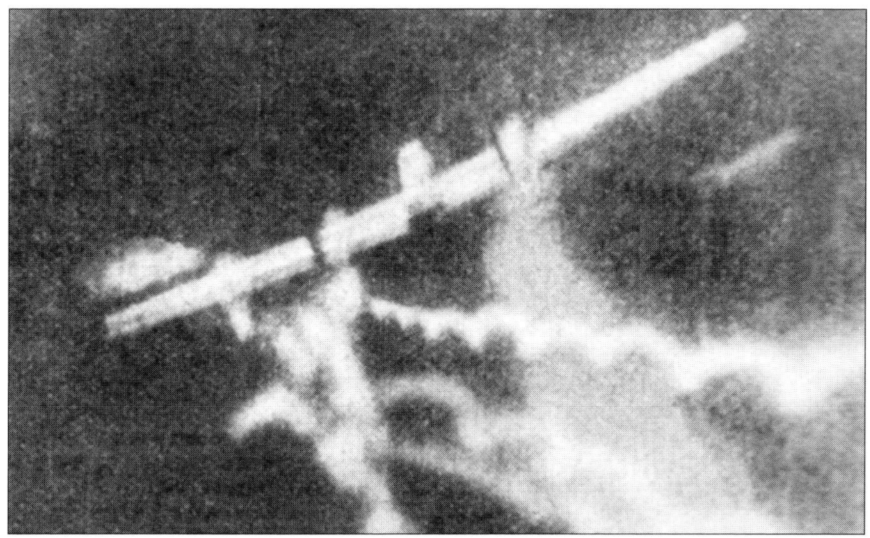

*Consecutive shots from the camera guns loaded into a Hurricane show a
Messerschmitt Bf110 being shot down over the English Channel.*

In all the Defiants of 264 Squadron claimed to have shot down 37
Germans with one crew, pilot Nicholas Cooke and gunner Albert Lippett,
claiming an astonishing eight kills in a single afternoon. The figures were
later revised when it was realised that one German had been claimed by
two gunners on several occasions, but even so the squadron seems to have

A series of cartoons drawn by a pilot at RAF Manston during 1940 and used for various publications printed at the base. (Manston S&H Mem)

shot down thirty enemy aircraft, their only loss being one gunner and some minor damage to three aircraft. It was the most successful day's combat any squadron in Fighter Command would ever achieve.

Aerial combats raged deep into France as the RAF fighters sought to stop the German bombers reaching Dunkirk. On the last day of the evacuation 32 Squadron, flying Hurricanes out of Biggin Hill, were over Le Treport when they sighted seventeen Heinkel 111 bombers heading for Dunkirk. The Hurricanes dived to attack, with the first victory going to Flight Lieutenant Michael Crossley, who saw his target explode in a ball of flame, presumably as the bombs exploded. Diving down to clear the tumbling wreckage, Crossley pulled up sharply to find a second Heinkel right in his sights. He fired a long burst at extreme range and was delighted to see flames erupt from one engine. The bomber then turned over and began a vertical dive. Crossley now saw that the enemy formation had broken up and headed for a lone Heinkel at a lower altitude. He closed to point blank range before pushing the gun button, only to find he had run out of ammunition. In all 32 Squadron shot down seven of the bombers in as many minutes.

In the same combat, Pilot Officer Victor Daw downed two Heinkels and, on his way home, shot down a 109 which was diving to attack a damaged Hurricane of 32 Squadron that was limping home from the fray.

The temptation to go down after a lone German was great for any fighter pilot, but could prove fatal, as Flight Lieutenant James Davies of 79 Squadron almost found out later that same day. He spotted a 109, apparently returning alone from combat, and dived down to attack it. Too intent on his intended victim to notice what was going on behind him, Davies became aware of his danger only when a spray of bullets struck his aircraft.

Throwing his Hurricane into a climbing turn, Davies found himself faced by six aircraft that he did not recognise at all. The black crosses on the newcomers wings were only too clear, however, and Davies threw himself into an attack. One of the strange aircraft went down in flames and the others scattered, allowing Davies to put his nose down and race to safety. He later identified the aircraft as Heinkel 115 light bombers. These were, however, naval aircraft and German records later revealed that none was involved in the fighting over Dunkirk.

One man who was very much involved, though the matter was hushed up for years afterwards, flew over the Channel to Dunkirk in a Hurricane

The Messerschmitt Bf109 that was brought down over Margate on 24 July 1940.
The aircraft crash-landed in a field and the pilot survived, though he was badly
wounded. (RAF Manston Mus)

bearing the identification marks of a non-existent squadron. The men in on the secret could recognise the aircraft at a distance by its drooping undercarriage. The pilot in question was Air Vice Marshal Sir Keith Park, commander of 11 Group. He explained his flights as 'going to see for myself'. Even today it is not clear how many flights he made, but it was at least two, and probably more.

One pilot flying out of Kent who was lost over Dunkirk was, when he was shot down, a rather insignificant Squadron Leader on Spitfires, but he was later to be celebrated in book and film. His name was Roger Bushell, a former British skiing champion who, at 30 years of age, was rather old for the role of fighter pilot. He was to become a master organiser of escapes from prisoner of war camps. He began a few months after being shot down and got to within two miles of the Swiss border before being caught. In 1941 he got out again, escaping from a railway carriage while in transit to another camp, but was again caught.

In 1942 the Germans opened a new camp for POWs at Sagen, naming it Stalag Luft III. Bushell was among the hundreds of men sent there. He at once set up an escape committee and began plotting how to get out. After a few false starts, Bushell came up with the plan that would later become famous as *The Great Escape*.

On 24 March 1944 Bushell led a total of 74 officers out of the camp through a tunnel from one of the camp huts dug through the crumbling sand. It was an audacious plan. Three tunnels had been started. One was found by the Germans, the second collapsed and only the third was completed. Originally some 200 men had intended to get out, but that was not to be.

The unexpected breakout astonished the Germans. Thousands of guards were drafted in to patrol railway stations, bridges and other places where escapees might expect to be found. For weeks the transport system in Germany was disrupted by searches and security checks. Eventually three of the escapees got to Britain, two via Sweden and another by way of Spain. Of those recaptured, fifty were taken out in ones and twos by the Gestapo to be shot dead on the direct orders of Adolf Hitler himself. Bushell, as the main organiser, was one of the first to be killed.

After the war, the British sent an investigator, Wing Commander Bowes, to discover what had happened. After months of patient work he had established precisely how 46 of the 50 had died and had 16 men under arrest. Of the Gestapo men involved with the killings, fourteen were

Messerschmitt Bf 109

Type:	Single seat fighter
Engine:	1175 hp Daimler Benz DB601Aa
Wingspan:	32 ft 4 in
Length:	28 ft
Height:	8 ft 2 in
Weight:	Empty 4189 lb
	Loaded 5875 lb
Armament:	2 x 20mm cannon plus 2 x 7.9mm machine guns
Max speed:	348 mph
Ceiling:	34,450 ft
Range:	410 miles
Production:	35,000

When it joined the Luftwaffe as an operational fighter in the spring of 1937 the Messerschmitt Bf 109 was far and away the best fighter in the world. It was fast and nimble in combat, while its armament packed a mighty punch. The figures given above are for the E model, which entered service in 1938 and was the dominant model during the Battle of Britain. The earlier models B, C and D had been powered by less powerful engines and by 1940 were used only for training. The 109 was produced in a further ten models with different engines and armament, there even being a ground-attack model equipped with bombs. By 1943 the 109 was increasingly being outclassed by more modern fighters, but it stayed in production as it remained a reliable workhorse for the Luftwaffe.

hanged in 1947 and two received life sentences. But the organiser of the killings, Commandant Scharpwinkel had been captured by the Russians in 1945. As the British evidence against him mounted, the Russians suddenly announced that Scharpwinkel had died of some unspecified disease. Bowes believed that he had, in fact, donned a Russian uniform and a new name to use his considerable talents for the KGB.

Back in 1940, the Dunkirk evacuation ended on 3 June. In those nine days of frantic effort to get the British army home Fighter Command had

Supermarine Spitfire

Type:	Single seat fighter
Engine:	1030 hp Rolls Royce Merlin
Wingspan:	36 ft 10 in
Length:	29 ft 11 in
Height:	11 ft 5 in
Weight:	Empty 4810 lb
	Loaded 5844 lb
Armament:	8 x 0.303 machine guns in wings
Max speed:	355
Ceiling:	31,900 ft
Range:	575 miles
Production:	20,351

When the Spitfire entered service it was immediately recognised as being a revolution in aircraft design. With its all-metal cantilevered monoplane design, retractable undercarriage and eight-gun armament, the 'Spit' was the most modern and effective aircraft in the RAF. Pilots recognised its easy handling and superlative combat manoeuvrability and it quickly became the favourite of RAF Fighter Command. However, its sophisticated design made it less easy to maintain than other fighters, so the Spitfire was more often unable to fly than the Hurricane. The figures given above are for the Spitfire MkI, the standard variant during the Battle of Britain. It was later to be produced in eleven main marks, plus three naval variants, dubbed 'Seafires', and was the only pre-war Allied fighter to remain in production to the end of the war.

flown a staggering 2,739 sorties, with 106 aircraft shot down and many more returning damaged. The Luftwaffe lost 132 aircraft over Dunkirk, though the RAF at the time claimed 258, while admitting that several of those were 'probables' rather than 'definites'. In all 338,226 Allied soldiers were rescued from Dunkirk, though they had to leave all their trucks, artillery and tanks behind.

Of the RAF aircraft shot down, 52 pilots were killed, 12 wounded and eight captured. The rest returned home from Dunkirk with the army on board ships.

For the next three weeks the war focussed on continued fighting in France. Having eliminated the Allied pocket at Dunkirk, the Germans swung south to attack over the Somme. The French armies had been demoralised by the swift German dash to the sea. The renewed German onslaught shattered the French in days. By 21 June the Germans had overrun Paris and were almost as far south as Bordeaux. The French surrendered.

As Dowding had foreseen, Britain was now alone. The fate of Britain, and ultimately of the world, rested on the shoulders of the men of Fighter Command; and Kent was right in the front line.

Chapter 3

Slaughter of the Innocents

As the smoke cleared from Dunkirk and the panzers were surging across France, an American newspaper reporter was interviewing Air Vice Marshal Charles Blount, who had been commanding the RAF squadrons sent to France. Blount was now back in London and was being used by the British Ministry of Information to give the British side of recent events.

As the interview closed the American asked, 'What's going to happen when the French are beaten and the Germans can turn their whole air force on to this country?' Blount thought for a moment then said, 'They're going to get the shock of their lives.'

During the fighting over France the pilots of Fighter Command had been growing increasingly unhappy with their standard tactics, particularly when contrasted with those of the Luftwaffe. Although the British pilots had achieved much, there was no doubt that control of the air over France lay with the Germans. One feature all British pilots noticed was that the Germans would not press an attack home unless they had a clear advantage, preferring to break off if the British gained the upper hand. But there was more to it than this combat caution.

Fighter Command tactics had developed during the 1930s as modern variants of the First World War methods, but updated for the new faster fighters and larger, better-armed bombers. The basis of all RAF fighter

A squadron of Spitfires flies in close formation in the officially approved four Vic formation. By the time this photo was taken in August 1940 most squadrons had abandoned this grouping when entering combat.

tactics was the squadron of twelve aircraft. This was divided into two flights of six aircraft, each able to operate independently. Each flight was further divided into two sections of three aircraft, though this was for tactical sake and the sections were not expected to operate independently. It was set down that the sections would be in the 'Vic' formation with the aircraft in the centre ahead of the other two.

There were three basic types of attack authorised by Fighter Command. The No.1 Attack was for use by a flight or squadron against a lone enemy bomber. The fighters would form up in line astern, behind and below the enemy. The squadron leader attacked first, closing to 400 yards, firing a short burst and then peeling away to allow the next fighter to attack in similar fashion. The first fighter would then turn away and return to the rear of the line astern.

The No.2 Attack was for use by a flight attacking a formation of bombers. The flight would approach the enemy from the rear and the two sections would separate when about 800 yards from the enemy. Each section would then swerve outwards to approach the enemy from a rear flank. After closing to 400 yards and firing a burst, the sections would peel outwards and then return to repeat the manoeuvre.

The No.3 Attack envisaged a flight approaching a large formation of bombers from the rear, with the two sections in line abreast. Again the fighters were to close, fire and peel away.

The No.4 Attack envisaged that a squadron of turret fighters would fly alongside the enemy bomber formation and fire at them from the beam. This would break up the bomber formations, allowing the single-seat fighters to dart in and pick off the stragglers one at a time.

It should be noted that the optimum firing range was set at 400 yards, since it was thought that this provided a sensible balance between the accuracy of the guns and the ability of a pilot to react at the combat speeds of a Hurricane fighter. The machine guns in the wings of all RAF fighters were angled so that the streams of bullets they fired would meet at a single point 400 yards in front of the aircraft.

The tactics worked well enough in peacetime practice combats, but they did rely on two very big assumptions. The first was that the enemy bombers would behave as the RAF trained its own bomber squadrons to behave. This was to fly straight and level in a tight formation so that the defensive guns of each aircraft could cover the next. The second assumption was that there would be no escorting fighters. Given the

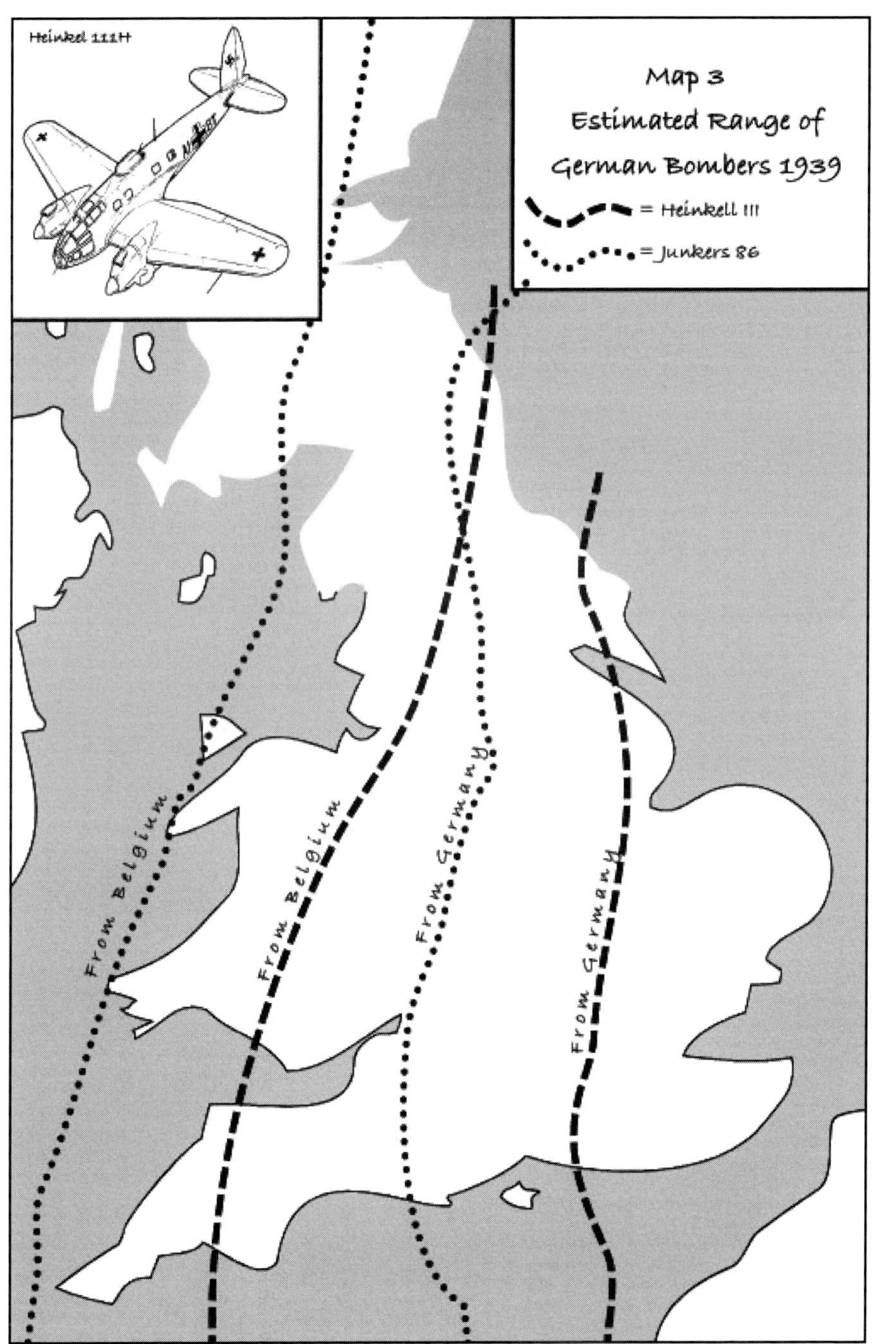
Heinkel 111H
Map 3
Estimated Range of
German Bombers 1939
= Heinkell III
= Junkers 86
From Belgium
From Belgium
From Germany
From Germany

distance from Germany to England, this latter was a reasonable premise, but, as the fighting over Dunkirk showed, the German fighters were actually based at mobile airfields close to the front line and very few Luftwaffe bomber formations went into battle without a fighter escort.

With France out of the war, the Luftwaffe now had the use of the well designed and well maintained French Air Force airfields. When the German bombers came, they would be escorted by fighters. Suddenly all the pre-war assumptions about bomber attacks on Britain were out of date.

There were other problems too. Many fighter pilots found that trying to open fire at 400 yards was unrealistic. At that range the relative speeds of aircraft whirling in combat made it almost impossible to estimate deflection – the position that a target aircraft will be in by the time the bullets reach it. It was much easier to open fire at 200 yards, or even 100 yards, when the enemy would have less time to move out of the way of a bullet stream. However, with the guns calibrated to converge at 400 yards the result was a peppering of the enemy rather than a concentrated funnel of bullets. Pilots increasingly demanded that their guns be recalibrated to shorter distances than those specified by the regulations.

The twisting vapour trails left by fighter aircraft engaged in a dogfight high above England. Such trails became a common sight as the Battle of Britain reached its height.

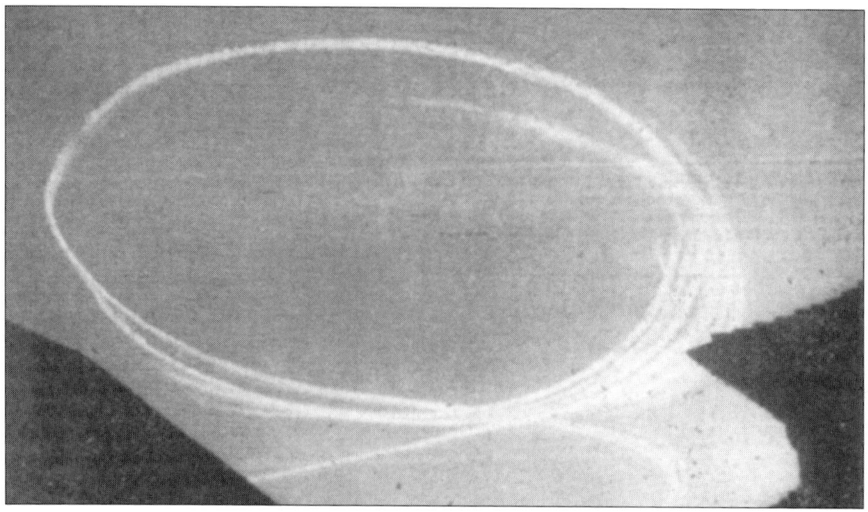

When it came to fighter vs fighter dogfights, the RAF pilots had learned that the Germans had a basic formation not of a squadron of twelve, but as a group of four – soon referred to as the 'finger four' because of the way the Germans formed up. This gave the German pilots a much more flexible approach to tactics, with fighters able to form up in multiples of four, even when those units were drawn from different squadrons. Moreover a single finger four would outnumber an RAF section in Vic formation with potentially disastrous results.

By the end of the Dunkirk operation most fighter squadrons in Kent were quietly dropping the pre-war tactics. Many had abandoned the section of three aircraft in Vic formation for a group of four fighters, in imitation of the Germans; others preferred to fly in pairs, with several groups of tightly formed pairs operating in a loose gaggle formation. It was now widely recognised that there would be time for only one attack on a formation of bombers before the escorting fighters intervened, so line ahead assaults were abandoned in favour of line abreast attacks. It had also been realised that the German bombers were poorly equipped with forward-facing guns, so attacks from head-on became preferred to the conventional attacks from behind.

All these changes were being introduced informally at squadron level and in many cases had not been adopted by many units. The official

A Spitfire has its guns tested by firing into an earthen bank. It was essential for success in combat for the guns to be aimed so that the lines of fire crossed at the correct position in front of the aircraft.

Unteroffizier Fritz Buchner of the Luftwaffe's Fighter Squadron No.3 poses with his Messerschmitt Bf109. Buchner was shot down and killed by Flying Officer Ken Marston of 56 Squadron, flying out of Manston on 26 August 1940. Buchner and his aircraft were buried 40 feet deep in the soil and his remains were not recovered until 1984. His family travelled to England to attend the funeral service, conducted with full military honours provided by the modern German air force. (Manston S&H Mem)

Fighter Command regulations remained unaltered. It was with the tactics in a state of flux that the men of Fighter Command in Kent now had to face the undivided attentions of the Luftwaffe.

Not that Dowding was ignoring the experiences of his pilots completely. On 21 June Squadron Leader Hunter of 264 Squadron had been called up to London to discuss the best tactics for the use of the Defiants of his squadron. Also present was Squadron Leader W. Richardson of 141 Squadron, another Defiant unit, which was then being moved to Hawkinge.

An aerial photo of Boulogne taken by an RAF reconnaissance aircraft in September 1940. The vast majority of the craft to be seen are barges brought from the Rhine that were intended to be used to transport infantry during the German invasion of Britain.

The day-long discussions were detailed and wide-ranging. It was eventually agreed that the Defiant needed two forward-firing guns to be effective against German fighters, but that until these could be fitted Defiants would be used only against bombers.

For the coming campaign Reichsmarshal Hermann Goering, the head of the Luftwaffe, had gathered a mighty force. In northern France was Luftflotte (Air Fleet) 2 while north-eastern France, Belgium and the Netherlands were home to Luftflotte 3. Between the two forces they could muster 875 bombers, 316 divebombers and 929 fighters. In Norway and Denmark was Luftflotte 5, with 123 bombers, but no fighters. To counter this force RAF Fighter Command had a total strength of just 650. Many of these aircraft were held back as local defence fighters over cities such as Birmingham or Newcastle, so only a fraction were available to front line units, mostly in Kent, Sussex and Essex.

The month of July was spent by the Luftwaffe principally bombing convoys of ships in the North Sea and English Channel, and attacking coastal naval targets. Goering was testing and probing at British defences, while keeping his own aircraft as close to base as possible. The German army was reorganising itself after the conquest of France to prepare for the invasion of Britain, while the German navy was gathering the ships that would be necessary to carry the army across the Channel. Once the navy and army were ready, the Luftwaffe would have the task of achieving air superiority by crushing the RAF, but that was for the future.

The Germans did not confine their attacks to naval targets; anything near the coast was fair game to their planners. Sitting on the Isle of Thanet, RAF Manston was a suitable target, and on 3 July it was hit by its first raid. This was a hit-and-run attack by a small group of Dorniers, which succeeded only in destroying the base's grass mowing machine.

Dowding, by contrast, kept his fighters on Ten ground as much as possible. He knew that the main battle was still to come and sent them up only when a vital target needed defending or a tactical advantage was clear. An exception was made on 7 July when 79 Squadron took off from Hawkinge to conduct a patrol over the ports of north-eastern France to gather data on German invasion preparations.

As the squadron roared over the Abbeville area Sergeant Alfred Whitby spotted a curious little aircraft scuttling along at low altitude far below them. Diving down to investigate he saw a single-engined aircraft with a broad, high wing and fixed undercarriage. The black cross was clear, so

Bombs fall around a convoy in the English Channel while Stuka divebombers fly overhead. Attacks by Stukas on convoys provoked many aerial combats during July and August 1940.

Whitby opened fire. The mysterious aircraft folded up in flight and crashed into the ground.

Only later did it become clear that Whitby had shot down a Henschel 126, a light transport aircraft with a startlingly short take-off run. It was favoured by senior German officers for hops around the country, as its short take off and landing runs meant it could be put down in small fields close to units or places the officer wished to visit. When they heard the news British intelligence wondered which senior officer had been cut down by Whitby, but after the war it turned out the aircraft had been on its way to a pick up and that only the pilot had been killed.

The next day seven Spitfires of 610 Squadron were ordered off from Biggin Hill to intercept a German bomber force that was attacking a British naval destroyer. The squadron had only seven aircraft fit to fly, due to damage sustained in an action earlier that day. That fight had ended with the squadron commander, Squadron Leader 'Big Bill' Smith nursing

Photographed by a press man standing on the South Coast this Spitfire swoops down low over the sea, from which projects the tail of a Messerschmitt Bf109 that the British pilot has just shot down.

Smoke pouring from an engine, a Heinkel 111 limps southward. Damaged aircraft such as this became a common sight crash-landing back onto Luftwaffe bases in northern France during 1940.

his crippled Spitfire home and landing at Biggin Hill, only for the aircraft to explode before he could escape.

In command on this second mission of the day was Flight Lieutenant John Ellis, the most senior officer fit for duty at the time. Despite his comparatively junior rank, Ellis handled the squadron with skill. They found the Heinkel 111s, which were guarded by 20 Messerschmitt 109s. Undaunted by the odds of more than 2:1 against them, the British pilots attacked the German fighters.

'I must have taken the enemy by surprise,' Ellis wrote later, 'as they did not break up or adopt any evasive action except a gentle turn. My target rolled over and plunged straight down towards the sea, out of control. As I climbed into the clouds I saw the 109 hit the sea. After this action I cruised around and sighted another section of four Me109s in line astern. I dived down below this section and carried out again a climbing attack on the last enemy aircraft. I emptied the remainder of my ammunition into him at point-blank range, and he fell out of the sky, burning furiously, and hit the sea.'

In all eight Germans were seen to go down in this action.

Not everyone was as careful to note his victories as Ellis. Pilot Officer Peter Gardner of 32 Squadron was asked at the end of July to assist an intelligence officer by cross checking the squadron records. When asked how many aircraft he had shot down, he replied 'Four in France and since returning to Britain five, or possibly more.' His total count was actually thought to be about fourteen, but he had been too busy to claim them. John McGrath of 601 Squadron was equally offhand. His commanding officer had him marked down as having destroyed twelve German aircraft by the end of July, but he himself had claimed only four.

Meanwhile the aerial fighting continued to quicken its pace. On 4 July the Germans had tried a new tactic, one that they were to use extensively in the weeks that followed. This was to become known to the pilots of Fighter Command as 'free chasing'. It involved sending over two or three squadrons of fighters at low altitude to tear across the English countryside, shooting at anything that moved. On this occasion 32 Squadron were sent up to intercept, but only managed to catch up with the Germans as they were heading back to France. In a short scrap one Hurricane was damaged, but no German aircraft were hit.

The free chasers were back at dawn on 8 July. British radar saw them coming, so 79 Squadron was scrambled from Hawkinge and 74 Squadron

A wounded German pilot shot down in August 1940 is given first aid while awaiting the arrival of a military ambulance to take him off to captivity.

from Manston. The Germans were over Hawkinge as the Hurricanes were taking off and managed to cause two to crash as they taxied. The men from Manston had better luck, shooting down one 109. The German pilot, Albert Stiberny, thus had the unfortunate distinction of being the first German fighter pilot to be shot down over England and captured.

On 9 July the Spitfires of 54 Squadron, operating temporarily from Manston, attacked bombers targeting a convoy in the Channel. One of the Germans was badly damaged and went down to execute a forced landing on the only bit of dry land within sight. Unfortunately for the German crew this turned out to be the Goodwin Sands. They were rescued by the grinning sailors of a Royal Navy patrol boat as the tide came in to submerge the sandbanks.

According to later historians studying documents with the aid of hindsight, the Battle of Britain officially began on 10 July. At the time, the

fighter pilots of Kent saw little change. The day was taken up with beating off German attacks on a convoy moving past Dover. On 12 July the weather closed in and flying was rendered impossible for almost a week.

On 19 July a force of German divebombers attacked a convoy off Folkestone. No.141 Squadron was scrambled from Hawkinge to drive them off. Of the 12 Defiants on the squadron strength, three were under repair, so only nine fighters actually got into the air. Unknown to the men of 141 Squadron, for the British radar had for once failed to spot them, the German bombers were being escorted by a squadron of 109s flying at 10,000 ft.

The German fighters were not only higher than the Defiants, but also up-sun of them. It was not until the diving 109s were just 2,000 ft above them and closing fast that they were spotted by Flight Lieutenant M. Loudon, who shouted a warning over his radio to his comrades. Seconds later, the Germans opened fire as they flashed past. One Defiant exploded and a second went down in flames. A third was damaged, at which the gunner bailed out to be lost at sea below, though the pilot, Pilot Officer J. MacDougall, managed to nurse his crippled aircraft back to Hawkinge.

The Messerschmitts were now climbing out of their dives to curve back and deliver another attack on the scattered Defiants. Loudon was hit first. His engine burst into flames and lost power instantly. By superb airmanship he managed to glide his stricken Defiant back to England, crash-landing into a field. Both he and his gunner were injured, but got out of the blazing wreckage alive. Another Defiant tried to crash-land, but exploded as it hit the ground. A sixth Defiant went down at some point, but none of the surviving British airmen saw it go.

At this point the Hurricanes of 111 Squadron, which had been patrolling nearby, tore into the fray. The leader had already seen two of the German aircraft fall away from the fight, though whether the Defiant gunners had shot them down or merely damaged them was unclear. Now two more 109s went down, this time definitely destroyed by the Hurricane guns.

In a short combat 141 Squadron had lost six of nine aircraft for no confirmed enemy losses. Dowding at once ordered them and 264 Squadron to be pulled out of the front line and sent north to where they faced only bombers coming from Norway or Denmark without fighter escort. It seemed that the days of Defiants flying from Kent were over – but fate had a strange card yet to play.

Taken in July 1940, this photo shows a Spitfire circling overhead as a damaged Messerschmitt Bf109 leaves Folkestone Harbour. The German aircraft subsequently splashed down and the pilot was rescued. (Manston S&H Mem)

On 24 July a massed dogfight developed over Margate as a large escort of German fighters pounced on British fighters attacking a force of Dornier bombers, which in turn were attacking a convoy. Six Messerschmitt 109s were shot down for the loss of only one RAF pilot killed, though others were injured. The incident was notable, as it was the first time that the German ace Adolf Galland entered the fray.

At this date Galland was already a legend in the Luftwaffe. He had spent the pre-war years pushing the importance of rigorous training for all air crew. On one occasion when he was practising low-level cross-country flying, he collided with a lamp post, but escaped with only concussion. By the time he entered the Battle of Britain as commander of a fighter squadron, he had already shot down twelve aircraft over Poland and Belgium. He had not achieved this without cost. On 21 June he had been shot down twice over France, both times parachuting down behind German lines and returning to his squadron.

At the end of July, Galland was awarded the Knight's Cross by Hitler, who added the coveted Swords in 1941. Galland took this opportunity to have a private word with the Führer. He asked Hitler if the propaganda broadcasts could stop insulting the RAF, since they were brave men doing a difficult job. Hitler refused to speak to the ace pilot for over a year.

Galland fought right through the war, shooting down 104 enemy aircraft and flying his final mission just a week before Germany surrendered. After the war he contacted and made friends with several British pilots, including those he had fought against in the skies over Kent

---

The blazing wreckage of a Dornier bomber brought down by an RAF fighter in August 1940.

during the Battle of Britain. He particularly delighted in inviting them to join him in wild boar hunts on his country estate in northern Germany.

By the end of the month, Dowding had realised the true reason for the German's free-chasing tactic. It had nothing to do with the damage the fighters were able to inflict on ground targets with their machine guns. In fact this was just a ruse to get the RAF fighters up into the air. Goering wanted to grind down the strength of Fighter Command before the invasion campaign even began.

Dowding was losing 80 fighter aircraft a week. While some pilots landed unscathed and returned to their squadrons, most were either killed or wounded and so were out of the fight, at least temporarily. Dowding ordered that the free-chasers were no longer to be intercepted. He could not afford the losses. It was a hard lesson that had been learned at the cost of much blood, but at least the British were learning. This was just as well, considering what was to come.

Another German tactic led to diplomatic moves at the highest levels by way of neutral governments. Several fighter pilots operating out of Manston came back to say that a German seaplane painted white and carrying the Red Cross insignia was stooging about in the convoy shipping lanes. At first it was assumed that the aircraft was on missions to pick up

The German flying boat that was forced down by pilots of Fighter Command after it was seen to be scouting out Allied convoys for bomber attack instead of rescuing downed airmen, as was its official mission. The misuse of the Red Cross symbol in this way caused a huge fuss at the time. (Manston S&H Mem)

Luftwaffe aircrew who had ditched in the sea, and it was left alone. But it gradually dawned on the intelligence officers at Bentley Priory that this aircraft was always being seen near convoys, never near downed German aircraft. The suspicion grew that the aircraft's mission was to report back on convoy positions rather than to rescue German fliers.

The British government approached neutral governments and asked them to pass on a protest to the Germans, the recognised method of communicating during wartime. The Germans ignored the messages. The British even suggested a way by which pilots of opposing forces could alert each other to aircrew in the sea. The Germans refused to reply and the suspect aircraft continued flying. Dowding reluctantly ordered that it should be shot down next time it was seen, which it was by Spitfires out of Biggin Hill.

There were, of course, many aircrew on both sides who found themselves 'in the drink', as they called ending up in the sea. Patrol boats and seaplanes from both sides were kept busy darting back and forth trying to rescue their own men, or to capture the enemy's. A contemporary newspaper reported the story of Pilot Officer Ward, a New Zealander flying with an unnamed squadron out of Kent who was regarded as very lucky by his messmates after bringing his Hurricane back to base in a crippled condition on several occasions. Then, one day in July, he did not come back and his comrades assumed his luck had finally run out. Several days later Ward arrived back at base. He had been shot down, and then picked up by a British patrol boat.

Unfortunately, he had taken off in such haste that he left behind his identity card and papers. The suspicious naval staff who greeted him at Dover thought he might be a German spy and so arrested him. It was two days before Ward was able to convince the hassled and very busy naval staff at Dover to contact Fighter Command direct, and even then it was another day before an air officer came down to take him back to his base for identification.

As soon as he was allowed back on flying duties, Ward got out a paint brush and decorated his Hurricane with a fictitious coat of arms sporting such omens of bad luck as a broken mirror, a person walking under a ladder, a match lighting three cigarettes and the number 13. Underneath he wrote 'So What The Hell'.

Such was the spirit of the men of Fighter Command in Kent as they faced their sternest test.

*The spoof coat of arms painted on to one Kent fighter by its pilot, Ward,
who had survived a run of bad luck and so professed to pay no heed
to other omens of bad luck.*

Boulton Paul Defiant

Type:	Twin seat turret-fighter
Engine:	1030 hp Rolls Royce Merlin
Wingspan:	39 ft 4 in
Length:	35 ft 4 in
Height:	12 ft 2 in
Weight:	Empty 6150 lb
	Loaded 8600 lb
Armament:	4 x 0.303 machine guns in dorsal turret
Max speed:	303 mph
Ceiling:	30,350 ft
Range:	465 miles
Production:	1075

The idea of a turret-fighter was born in 1933, when powered gun-turrets entered production for bombers. During the first World War twin-seat fighters had performed well, the mobility of their rear twin guns operated by a gunner giving them a murderous field of fire that made them ideal aircraft to escort bombers, or to attack those of the enemy. It was hoped that the additional firepower of four guns mounted in a turret that could quickly spin around to face a new direction would make the new generation of turret-fighters highly effective in combat. The Defiant was the result, entering service in December 1939. After some initial successes, the Defiant proved to be too cumbersome and slow to deal with fast modern fighters. It was then modified to take air-to-air radar and converted into a night-fighter, in which role it proved to be highly successful. By 1942 purpose-built night-fighters entered service, and the Defiant was relegated to training duties and testing new equipment.

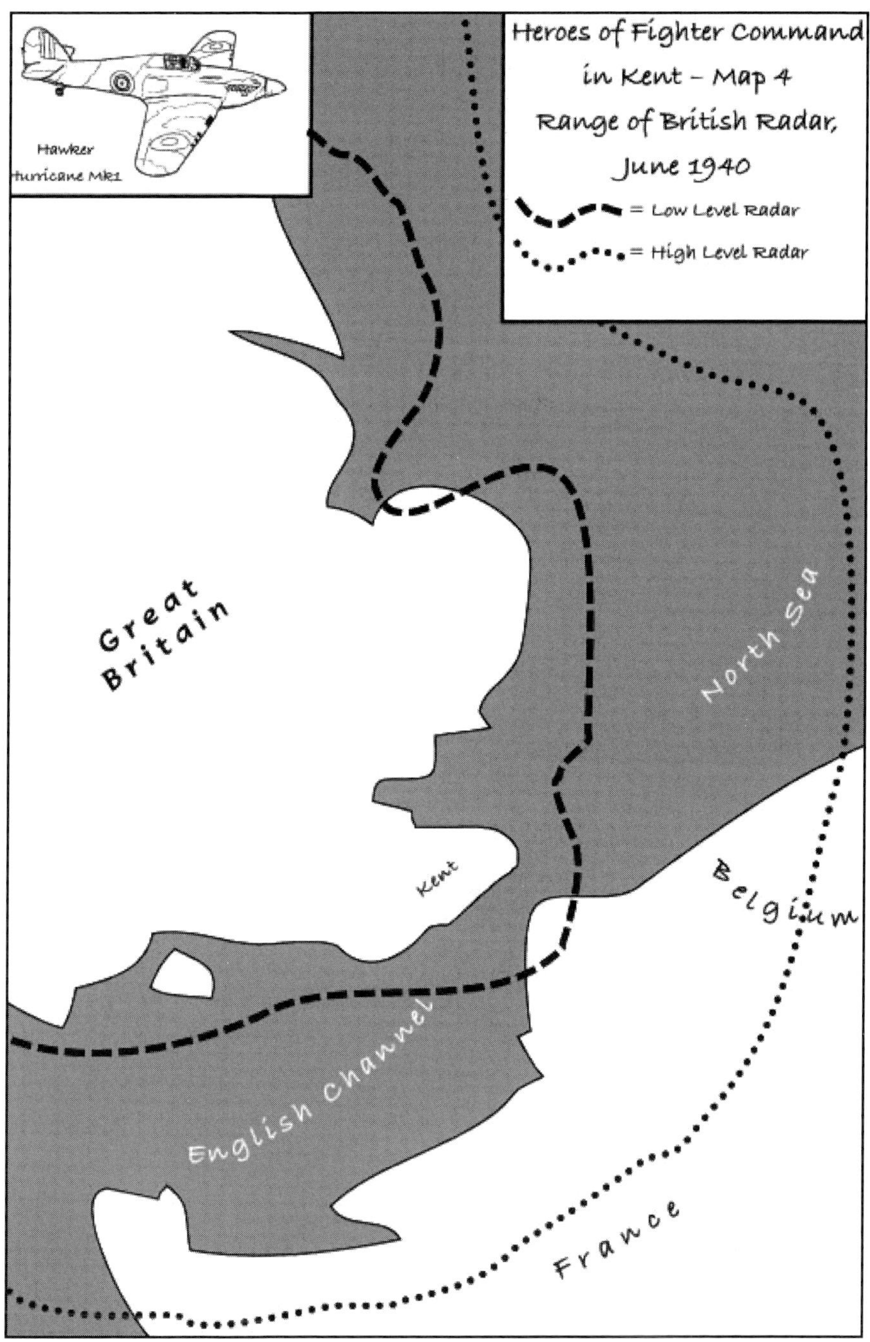

Hawker
Hurricane Mk1
Heroes of Fighter Command
in Kent – Map 4
Range of British Radar,
June 1940
= Low Level Radar
= High Level Radar
Great
Britain
North Sea
Kent
Belgium
English Channel
France

Chapter 4

Hellfire Corner

In June 1940 the radio listening posts that the Germans had set up in northern France to eavesdrop on British military radio signals reported that on certain wavelengths they were picking up the most peculiar signals. It was early July before a scientist at Luftwaffe HQ in Berlin recognised them as being radar. The Germans were by this date developing their own radar system, based largely on captured French sets, but even so they did not fully appreciate the importance of radar to the British air defence system. Such errors of intelligence were to prove crucial in the month of August 1940.

Not only did the Germans think that British radar was able to pick up their aircraft only when they were close to the British coast, they also thought it could not detect an aircraft flying at under 500 ft – neither of which was true.

The pre-war general intelligence that the Germans had acquired on the RAF – known in the Luftwaffe as the Blue Study – was excellent. It contained accurate data regarding the location of aircraft factories as well as RAF bases and civil airfields that could be converted to military use, and most such places had been photographed from the air by German civil aircraft. There was also an accurate estimation of RAF strength both in peacetime and when fully mobilised for war.

Once the war got underway, however, the Germans found themselves

The Hurricane production line at Hawker's factory. The ability of the British aircraft industry to pour out replacement fighters amazed the Germans.

cut off from any up-to-date information that could not be gained from aerial photographs. Thus the entirely accurate pre-war estimate of maximum fighter production of 200 aircraft per month was not updated to take account of the emergency factory expansion programme that, at the commencement of the Battle of Britain, was turning out 460 fighters per month. The British could replace losses much faster than the Germans thought they could.

Similarly, the Germans tended to write off an airbase after it had been bombed. This was the result of experience in both Poland and France, where the pressures caused by rapidly advancing German army units meant that the air forces of those countries had not been able to repair their airbases once damaged and get them operational again. Britain, though, was able to get even the most devastated airfield back into operation again within a few days. The British habit of filling in only those bomb craters that were blocking the runway misled the Germans who analysed aerial photos. They saw airfields pockmarked by bomb craters and assumed this meant they had not been repaired when, in fact, they had.

These factors came into effect slowly during August, but by September were becoming serious. Goering's strategy was based on his intelligence reports, and those proved to be faulty. For the men of Fighter Command in Kent, however, such high level intelligence matters were somewhat academic. So far as they were concerned throughout that August of glorious sunny weather the only thing that really mattered was that the German aircraft formations kept on coming, and they kept on coming in vast numbers.

The first two weeks of the month saw little change in the pattern of Luftwaffe raids. They continued to hit convoys and coastal targets, with free-chasing formations of fighters pushing deeper inland, though these

A Luftwaffe publicity photo from October 1940 shows Junkers Ju88 bombers on their way to bomb England.

were generally ignored. The sheer number of German aircraft coming over was, however, gradually increasing.

During this hectic period the normal administrative life of Fighter Command had to continue – the men and women had to be fed and paid amid the mayhem of war. One key duty was the award of medals for the fighting men. It was considered essential to morale that bravery in action or consistent dedication to duty should be seen to be rewarded.

It was therefore with some frustration that the commanding officer of 501 Squadron picked up his pen on 6 August and wrote to Fighter Command HQ. 'Sergeant James Lacey, No.740042,' he wrote 'was recommended on 27 June, 1940, through Headquarters, for an award of the DFM (Distinguished Flying Medal), but it is thought that his recommendation must have been mislaid or lost. Since that date he has shot down one more enemy aircraft, taking his total to six. The recommendation is again submitted, as I quote "This NCO took part in most patrols flown by the squadron. He shot down five enemy aircraft and shared a sixth. In action, he showed determination and coolness and was a valuable asset to his squadron".'

This time no chances were being taken. A phone call was put through to Dowding's office and the situation explained to him. Dowding took time out from his busy life to scribble a handwritten note and have it sent down to the medals section. It read 'I understand that this NCO was recommended for an award for services in France, but this may have been mislaid. He has now shot down six enemy aircraft and has shown determination and coolness. I therefore recommend him for the immediate award of the Distinguished Flying Medal.' The medal was awarded without delay.

Dowding may have been nicknamed 'Stuffy' but he knew what was important to his men and they loved him for it.

As it turned out this was not the last that Dowding would hear of Sergeant James Lacey. On 2 November 1940 a report would land on his desk advising him that Lacey had reached the figure of twenty enemy aircraft confirmed as destroyed. Once again Dowding picked up his pen and sent a personal note to those whose job it was to award medals. 'I strongly recommend this gallant young pilot for a Bar to his Distinguished Flying Medal,' read the note. Lacey got it.

On 1 August Hitler had received assurances from his army commanders that the ground forces would be ready to invade Britain by the first week

*A fighter pilot makes his post-combat report to the squadron intelligence officer.
The number of enemy aircraft encountered, how many damaged or shot down and
their types were the prime consideration.*

of September. The naval chiefs were not so confident in their estimates, but thought that their ships would be ready by the second week of September. Both, however, specified that they would not be able to guarantee success if the Royal Navy were free to attack the invasion fleet. That meant that the Luftwaffe had to have control of the skies over the English Channel so that it could bomb the British ships at will. All eyes turned to Goering and the Luftwaffe.

On 1 August Goering held a top-level conference with his strategic planners and senior Luftflotte commanders to discuss the problem of how to crush the RAF. Although they were working with faulty information, the Luftwaffe bosses came up with a workable and practical plan. They would launch heavy, concentrated bombing raids on the radar stations and bases of RAF Fighter Command, especially those south of the Thames. The aim was to knock them out of action and so render RAF Fighter Command ineffective. Goering ordered his planners to prepare detailed target assessments and bomb-aiming points to ensure maximum damage. That would take a few days, so it was decided that the massed assault would begin on 13 August.

Goering dubbed it Adlertag – 'Eagle Day'. It was bad luck for him that 13 August was a day of cloud and poor visibility, so only some of the planned raids took place. Nevertheless, the radar station on the Isle of Wight was knocked out, while Manston and Hawkinge were both put out of action.

Manston was hit at 12.50 while 65 Squadron was on the ground being refuelled after an earlier action. The pilots raced for their aircraft and all but one got airborne amid the exploding bombs. They were unable to land back at Manston, however, and the airfield was out of action for more than a day.

Michael Crossley, a pilot with 610 Squadron out of Biggin Hill was nursing his crippled Spitfire back to base when his engine suddenly stopped. He had to get down quick and headed for Hawkinge. He called up Hawkinge on the radio and asked for permission to come down. 'We've had a spot of bother,' came back the laconic reply, 'but you are welcome to try.' Somehow Crossley got down without crashing into a bomb crater and next morning was up again with his squadron in a new Spitfire.

One raid that did go ahead on Eagle Day was an attack soon after dawn on Dungeness by a force of Dornier 215s, escorted by 109s. No.610

An Observer Corps post in August 1940. Each post was protected by sandbags and was manned permanently by two men, linked to a regional headquarters by phone. The observers were responsible for positive identification of enemy aircraft types and numbers as well as plotting their movements once they crossed the coast.

Squadron from Biggin Hill went up to intercept. A savage dogfight resulted, though the swirling combat happened so fast that the men of 610 were uncertain if they had shot down ten Germans or none at all. They did know that Pilot Officer Ted 'Smithy' Smith was missing when they got back to 'The Bump'.

Smith's Spitfire had been hit early in the battle. The aircraft dived towards the sea with smoke pouring from the engine. Worried that the smoke would turn to flames, Smith decided to bail out, but the aircraft was by this point diving so fast that the wind pressure was holding the canopy shut. By now totally blinded by choking smoke, Smith pulled back on the joystick to level off and, as soon as the aircraft slowed, threw open the canopy. He leapt clear, but could see nothing and pulled the ripcord after what he judged was enough time to get clear of the stricken aircraft. He was still trying to clear his eyes of smoke when he hit the sea. A passing fishing boat pulled him out of the drink and took him back to England.

Pilots of 29 Squadron relax between missions in the summer of 1940. The squadron was flying Blenheim Mk1 aircraft at this date.

The weather on 14 August was even worse, but 15 August dawned clear and bright. Over 500 German bombers took off for England that morning, escorted by 600 fighters. They pounded RAF targets across southern England, with Kent's Hawkinge and Lympne being particularly badly hit, as was the Shorts aircraft factory at Rochester. The Luftwaffe was back in the afternoon to bomb more aircraft factories and that evening returned to concentrate their attentions on the RAF.

The Germans came back the next day in huge numbers, slackened off on 17 August because of poor weather, and then redoubled their efforts on 18 August, when Biggin Hill was pounded badly.

One German bomber came to an unusual end that day. The Dornier 17 piloted by Rudolf Lamberty was attacking Biggin Hill at low level when one of his gunners spotted a Spitfire coming down to attack from behind. Lamberty began to make evasive manoeuvres, but before the Spitfire had even opened fire he saw flames erupting from the fuel tank in the fuselage. Struggling with the controls, Lamberty managed to put his bomber down in a nearby field. He and his crew scrambled out, and were at once arrested by a squad of what they thought were soldiers.

Issued by the government in August, this photo shows the pilots of an unidentified Spitfire squadron 'somewhere in southern England, ready for immediate call to action'.

The men were, in fact, the 4th Platoon of the Kent Home Guard, who that day were on duty guarding the approaches to Biggin Hill in case the long-expected German invasion began with a paratroop drop to seize the airfield. Lamberty was amazed to discover that his aircraft had been brought down by a volley fired by the antiquated First World War rifles of the Home Guard. Lieutenant Bertie Miller had ordered his men to fire the volley as the German streaked overhead and one lucky bullet must have found a vulnerable spot in the Dornier's fuselage.

One of the pilots based at Biggin Hill that day, Flying Officer John Humpherson of 32 Squadron, had already been bombed out of a base during the fighting in France and had two German aircraft to his credit when the bombs rained down on Biggin Hill. 32 Squadron was up fighting another force of German bombers when the raid took place. Humpherson downed two more Germans, and would later raise his score to six, but was once again unable to land at base and was diverted to a forward landing ground. His celebrations had to wait.

Another pilot whose celebrations were not held straight away, though this time due to his injuries, was Pilot Officer John Gibson of 501 Squadron, based temporarily at Biggin Hill as the crisis struck. He was ordered to take his Hurricane to intercept a force of Junkers Ju87 Stuka divebombers that were heading for the radar station just outside Dover. The Germans were found at high level before they began their dive and Gibson joined his comrades in the attack. He had the satisfaction of seeing one Stuka go down before his guns, when suddenly his engine shuddered under the impact of cannon shells and then erupted into flames.

Gibson threw back his canopy and got ready to jump, when he realised that his aircraft was in a steep dive aiming straight for the centre of Folkestone. Dropping back into his seat, Gibson wrestled with the controls in a desperate effort to steer the blazing craft away from the helpless civilians in the town below. Not until the burning Hurricane was down to 1,000 ft and heading towards open country did Gibson finally jump. His parachute opened and he floated down to the ground. He had suffered some slight burns in his adventure, but had probably saved several lives.

Another Biggin Hill pilot whose career was cut short by going down in flames was Douglas 'Grubby' Grice of 32 Squadron, who had eight German aircraft on his score sheet when he took off on the morning of 15 August 1940. His squadron was heading for Harwich, then being bombed by the Luftwaffe. As the Hurricanes approached Harwich, Grice spotted a force of Messerschmitt 110s high overhead, circling in their by now familiar defensive formation. He had just radioed the sighting to the squadron leader when disaster struck.

An incendiary bullet crashed through the canopy, shattered the instrument panel and plunged into the fuel tank. Grice had just long enough to register what had happened when the ruptured fuel tank caught fire. Flames streamed back to fill the cockpit and smother the unfortunate Grice. Events moved quickly, the Hurricane flipped on to its back and Grice fell free, dropping out of the flames and plunging headfirst through the empty air.

'I remembered my parachute drill and waited two seconds before I pulled the ripcord,' he later wrote. 'I was relieved to see I was over land, but the breeze soon carried me out to sea.' Grice came down gently enough into a calm sea and inflated his lifejacket. There he bobbed about for over an hour until a patrol boat, alerted to his position by his squadron comrades, came to fetch him.

Once in hospital, Grice feared the worst for the burns he had picked up, but he need not have worried. His facial burns healed remarkably quickly and completely, surprising the doctors in the RAF's burns unit which pioneered the techniques of plastic surgery. It was because of Grice's quick recovery that the unit began experimenting with saline washes, and found that a swift bath in salt water was the best treatment to be found for surface burns.

This was, in fact, the third time that Grice had been shot down. The first time had been over France, and the second time over Kent, on 4 July 1940. He had already won the DFC (Distinguished Flying Cross), receiving his medal from King George VI in person. Although his burns healed quickly, he was judged no longer fit to fly and so became Operations Room Controller at Biggin Hill. He later rose to the rank of wing commander, retiring from the RAF when peace came and going into commercial law as a career.

Biggin Hill was hit again on 18 August, but this time it was a woman who won a medal, not a man. WAAF Sergeant Elizabeth Mortimer had the task of ringing unexploded bombs with red flags. Pilots coming in to land could see bomb craters from the air and avoid them. Unexploded bombs (UXB) were too small to be seen, but could explode with fatal results if an aircraft landed on them.

Sergeant Mortimer had already marked a couple of UXBs and was approaching a third when it suddenly went off. She was thrown to the ground and severely winded. An officer came running over to see if she needed medical aid, but after a few minutes realised that she was not badly hurt. The officer ordered Mortimer to take cover, but she ignored him and continued until all the UXBs were marked. The pilots were able to land safely and Elizabeth Mortimer was later awarded a Military Medal for her work.

That bomb craters could be a real hazard was discovered to his apparent cost by Sergeant Ronald Hamlyn just after dawn on 23 August. The Spitfire had a notoriously long nose. This was not much of a problem in the air, but on the ground, with the aircraft angled upward, it meant the pilot had very little forward vision. Pilots were supposed to move forward in a series of sweeping turns so that the pilot could peer around the engine cowling. As he taxied out to take off on patrol, Sergeant Hamlyn omitted to do this and drove his Spitfire straight into a bomb crater. The undercarriage was wrecked and the propeller sheared off, so that it would take days to repair the aircraft.

Hamlyn was sent to report to the station commander for disciplinary action. He was standing in the commander's ante room when at 8.25 he heard the emergency scramble bell. Hamlyn raced from the room and

---

A Hurricane MkI has an unfortunate 'prang' at an undisclosed RAF Kent airfield, some time in 1940. (Manston S&H Mem)

leapt into the cockpit of the nearest Spitfire. He joined the squadron as they climbed towards Ramsgate to meet a formation of Junkers Ju88s escorted by 109s. Hamlyn shot down an 88, then sent a 109 spinning down out of control.

When the squadron landed, Hamlyn headed back to the commander's office for his disciplinary hearing. Barely had the meeting begun when the scramble signal sounded again. Hamlyn raced to leap into a Spitfire and took off at 11.35. This time the intruders were near Dover. Hamlyn got into a dogfight with a 109. When the German put his nose down and fled, Hamlyn followed. He finally caught up with the German over Calais, and sent him down into the sea.

For the third time Hamlyn reported for his hearing. This time the proceedings went ahead and the hapless pilot had just been found guilty of negligence on duty when the alert sounded once more. Following his comrades to the Isle of Sheppey, Hamlyn bagged two more German aircraft before returning to Biggin Hill.

This time Hamlyn returned to the station commander's office rather grubby and extremely tired. The senior officer sternly told him that he was being fined £5 (then a fair amount of money) for his crime – and that he was being recommended for the DFM. The medal was awarded immediately.

Goering held a meeting of his senior commanders on the 19 August. Their faulty intelligence had a serious impact on this meeting. The Germans thought that they had destroyed about half of Fighter Command, and so concluded that a few more days of targeting RAF bases would secure them the coveted control of the air. At the same time their own losses, particularly of bombers, was worryingly high. Goering ordered that in future escorting fighters had to stay close to the bombers at all times, not go off chasing likely looking targets. In addition the number of fighters flying escort was doubled, so that a force of 50 bombers might have as many as 120 fighters swarming around it.

The new German tactics came into force on 24 August and the effects were immediate and dramatic. RAF fighter combat losses soared as German losses dropped. On 18 August the Germans had lost 71 aircraft and the British 27. On 31 August the Germans lost 41 aircraft, the RAF 39. It was a rate of loss that Dowding knew he could not sustain. He was losing fighters twice as fast, and more importantly trained pilots three times as fast. German losses were higher, but they had more to lose. If

A German photo shows a Dornier Do17Z over Kent, the river is probably the Medway near Rochester. (Manston S&H Mem)

things carried on like this RAF Fighter Command would be destroyed within three weeks, while the Luftwaffe would still have half its original strength left.

It was on that 24 August when the Luftwaffe changed tactics that the Defiant turret-fighters returned to Kent. 264 Squadron had been sent to Manston with orders to patrol over the airfield and tackle any German bombers that tried to attack. They went into action at lunchtime, and shot down five Junkers Ju88s for the loss of one Defiant. When the escorting 109s came down, the Defiants did less well but still managed to shoot down two Germans for the loss of two of their own number.

That evening the seven Defiants still fit to fly went up to tackle a mixed formation of Ju88s and Heinkel 111s from below while a squadron of Spitfires drew off the German fighter escort. Flight Lieutenant George Garvin and his gunner shot down two Ju88s in less than a minute, but the Defiants had to break off when a formation of 109s came in to attack. A few days later the Defiants were moved to Essex. Once again, it seemed that Kent had seen the last of the turret fighters. Once again, fate decreed otherwise.

On 30 August a massed raid was sent by the Luftwaffe to smash the airfields of Kent. Flying Officer Teddy Morris of 610 Squadron was with his squadron when the commander chose to attack a formation of Heinkel 111s head on. The tactic could be devastating, as the Germans were poorly armed frontally, but it called for split-second timing, as the aircraft had a combined closing speed of almost 600 mph. Morris mistimed his turn and ploughed his Spitfire straight into the nose of a Heinkel. Astonishingly, he was thrown clear of the impact and parachuted safely to earth. It was not a mistake he made again.

Meanwhile, Biggin Hill was being hit by its heaviest raid so far. Numerous buildings were flattened, including sleeping quarters and the Naafi. The sector HQ was hit by a 500 lb bomb, which blew the roof off. Telephonist Helen Turner was on the line to 11 Group HQ when the bomb hit and the alarmed staff at Uxbridge heard the unfolding events over the telephone.

Two bomb shelters had received direct hits and, as soon as the German raiders were gone, rescue workers swarmed over the remnants of the shelters, both of which had collapsed. The first was beside the aircraft maintenance hangars and had been packed with ground crew. As the broken concrete and earth was heaved aside the gruesome fact that everyone inside had been killed became clear. Forty men had died. The

Fighter pilots at readiness while sitting outside a dispersal hut await the sound of the scramble bell. The summer of 1940 was glorious. (Manston S&H Mem)

second shelter was the one beside the WAAF quarters. Appalled by the death toll at the first shelter, the workers dug frantically. Astonishingly only one woman was dead, the rest had survived being buried under tons of earth.

Despite such damage and the worsening situation, the overall figures for August looked very positive for the British. With hindsight things were not as good as the official British figures showed. Many German bombers marked down as destroyed had in fact limped back to France. But nor were the conditions as bad as the German official figures painted them.

At this difficult time, Dowding found himself on the end of a volley of requests for confirmations, data and interviews from the world's neutral press. The Ministry of Information pressed him repeatedly to come to London and give interviews to the American press. Dowding refused, stating that he had too many more important things to do – such as saving Britain from invasion. In desperation a ministry official begged him for some sort of guarantee about the figures of aircraft losses for him to quote to the world's press.

'Tell them,' Dowding said down the phone from his office at Bentley

Heinkel 111

Type: Five crew medium bomber
Engine: 2 x 1200hp Junkers Jumo 211D-1
Wingspan: 74 ft 1 in
Length: 53 ft 9 in
Height: 13 ft 1 in
Weight: Empty 17,000 lb
Loaded 30,865 lb
Armament: 1 x 20mm cannon nose, 1 x 13 mm machine gun in dorsal position, 7 x 7.9 mm machine guns in ventral, beam and nose positions.
Bomb load: 7165 lb
Max speed: 252 mph
Ceiling: 21,980 ft
Range: 1280 miles
Production: 7300

The figures given above are for the Heinkel 111H, of which over 6000 were built. There were 11 other models, one of them a naval torpedo bomber, but these were only built in small numbers. The H was the sixth model in the series and the first to have the distinctive glazed nose. The 111 first entered service in 1936, the H model arriving in 1939. It was the mainstay of the Luftwaffe's bombing arm and was classified as a heavy bomber when it first appeared, though it is now generally reckoned to be a medium bomber in comparison to the Allied four-engined giants. The Luftwaffe remained primarily dedicated to helping the army by bombing military targets behind the front lines, plus the occasional terror raid, such as those on Warsaw and Rotterdam, to bully an enemy government into early surrender. In such roles the Heinkel 111 was supreme.

Priory, 'that if our figures are correct the Germans will give up. If the German claims are correct they will be in England within a week.'

Then Dowding hung up and went back to the fateful situation facing Fighter Command.

Chapter 5

London

The heavy losses suffered by RAF Fighter Command in the last week of August 1940 not only put great pressure on Dowding, but also brought to a head a simmering dispute between his two most senior officers – Air Vice Marshal Park in command of 11 Group and Air Vice Marshal Leigh-Mallory in charge of 12 Group.

Dowding's strategy until then had been based on maintaining fighter squadrons at bases south of the Thames to dispute German control of the air over the English Channel and to fend off German bombing attacks on RAF bases and other targets in the area. His prime concern had been to keep fighters in the air over Kent. He had, however, kept twenty fighter squadrons out of harm's way in northern England. Officially they were there to guard northern cities from German attack, but they were also seen by Dowding as a reserve force to be brought south when the German invasion began.

Faced by unsustainable losses, Dowding now had to consider abandoning Kent altogether. Much as he might want to protect the towns and military bases of the south from bombing attack, he was aware that his primary duty was to stop an invasion of Britain by the German army crossing the English Channel in ships. If all his fighters were destroyed before the invasion began, they would not be available to attack the German bombers seeking to sink the Royal Navy as it went out to do battle with the German invasion fleet.

Now Dowding seriously considered the option of pulling his squadrons back north of London. This would mean that they would be on bases out of range of the 109, so the Germans could reach them only with

A Blenheim Mk1 circles over a burning German merchant ship in the North Sea in March 1940. The fastest fighter in the RAF when it was introduced in 1937, the Blenheim was outclassed by the German fighters in 1940 and was soon moved out of the front line.

Photographed from the cliffs of the South Downs, a convoy moving west along the Channel comes under attack from German bombers.

unescorted, and therefore vulnerable, bombers. Such a move would undoubtedly save his men and machines from the ongoing losses. It would also lay the towns and cities of the south open to German bomber attack. Memories of the ruthless terror raids on Rotterdam and Warsaw were still fresh. Dowding did not want to see London, Canterbury or Chichester laid waste without offering some sort of defence.

It was a terrible dilemma that faced Dowding, one made all the worse by the disputes between Park and Leigh-Mallory.

The internal struggles that beset Fighter Command's higher echelons at this time have since become known as 'The Big Wing Controversy'. The disputes were in many ways complex and at times soured by personal animosities, but they can be reduced to a few interlinked disagreements.

Park believed in what might be termed an aggressive defensive strategy. He wanted to attack German formations as soon as they were spotted, scrambling the nearest squadron to go up and do battle. He argued that this forced the Luftwaffe onto the back foot. More importantly, it meant that the bomber formations were destroyed, broken up or at least disrupted before they reached their targets. Thus the damage the Germans were able to inflict was much reduced. The down side to such a strategy was that the first RAF fighter squadron to be scrambled very often found itself out numbered by the German fighters escorting the bombers.

Leigh-Mallory favoured what he termed the 'big wing'. Under this strategy the RAF fighters would be scrambled as the German bombers came over the coast, but instead of attacking them at once the fighters would move away out of sight of the intruders. There they would climb to gain the advantage of height over the Germans. When a 'wing' of three or more squadrons was assembled the force would be directed towards the Germans by radar controllers. This would put the RAF fighters into a much better position to attack the Germans and inflict heavier losses on them. The downside was that it would take so long to assemble the big wing that the Germans would have bombed their target unopposed, and might even have returned home, before the RAF fighters could attack.

Both strategies had advantages and disadvantages in theory and would have made for interesting staff discussions. The problem was that with the mighty Luftwaffe pounding southern England the time was for action, not theories. Throughout August, Dowding, wrestling with his own problems, had left Park and Leigh-Mallory to handle their commands as they saw fit. But the devastating raid on Biggin Hill on 30 August forced Dowding to get involved.

It had long been the case that, if Park had all his squadrons committed meeting raids coming in over 11 Group territory, he could ask Leigh-Mallory for help. And, if Leigh-Mallory did not have his hands full meeting German attacks coming in across East Anglia, he was obliged to send squadrons to cover areas specified by Park.

This arrangement had not been working well for some time. Leigh-Mallory, favouring the big wing, refused to allow his fighters to head south until at least three squadrons were in formation at high altitude. While the squadrons were forming up, the hard-pressed Park had either seen the Germans hit their target, or had diverted one of his squadrons to the attack. Thus when the 12 Group aircraft arrived the Germans were either on their way home and short of fuel – and therefore were unwilling to fight – or had already had their formations broken up by 11 Group fighters – and therefore were easy prey.

Leigh-Mallory's men began clocking up impressive tallies of downed German aircraft, encouraging Leigh-Mallory and his officers to broadcast the advantages of their big wing theory. Meanwhile, Park and his men grumbled that they had broken up the German formations and that their airfields had been bombed.

The Biggin Hill raid of 30 August proved to be crucial because it was the final straw for Park. That morning radar had picked up large numbers of German raids forming over northern France. Clearly it was going to be a very busy morning for 11 Group, so Park contacted Leigh-Mallory and asked him to use his squadrons to protect the 11 Group bases in Essex and northern Kent. So when a large German bomber force was located on radar heading for Biggin Hill, Park ignored it. He directed his squadrons elsewhere because he believed that Leigh-Mallory and 12 Group would deal with the raid heading for Biggin Hill.

Leigh-Mallory had, indeed, been alerted by the radar plots of the raid and had got his fighters into the air. But by the time the big wing had been formed and was heading south, Biggin Hill was a smoking wreck – as were several factories and other secondary targets. Dozens of servicemen and women had been killed, plus over 50 civilians. Not only had the German bombers reach Biggin Hill unmolested, they had got back to France without meeting a single RAF fighter. When the big wing did arrive, it caught another German raid heading for Essex and drove it off, shooting down nine Germans.

Leigh-Mallory claimed a victory for his big wing idea but Park was apoplectic with fury. Dowding now had to face an open and acrimonious row between his two most senior commanders, in addition to all his other problems. He called the two men to his office separately and listened to their grievances. Then he set about working out a method by which Leigh-Mallory would be forced to release individual squadrons if a threat to 11 Group bases was urgent, but which otherwise allowed him to form up his big wings.

The new arrangement did nothing to halt the acrimony and distrust between Park and Leigh-Mallory and the men who served them. Official complaints continued to be batted back and forth, but the overwhelming need to defeat the Germans and the enormous workload on the two men meant that they did not have too much time to devote to the controversy. All that would change once the immediate threat of invasion was over.

In the meantime, Leigh-Mallory sent for an officer in his command named Peter Macdonald, who was also an MP. Leigh-Mallory briefed Macdonald thoroughly on his big wing ideas and his view of events to date. Macdonald would later talk long and earnestly on the subject to other MPs and ministers when he was at Westminster. At the time neither Park nor Dowding knew anything about Macdonald's activities. No doubt Macdonald thought he was merely passing on useful information, but when Dowding found out about it years later, he viewed it as part of a plot by Leigh-Mallory to go behind Dowding's back and get his own way.

Such controversies were, however, unknown to the pilots of Fighter Command in Kent. Their concern was with the Luftwaffe and its seemingly unending supplies of men and machines.

Park now extended the so called 'aerodrome guard' system. This involved one fighter from each base circling high overhead at all times so that Germans attacking airfields would meet at least some opposition and might, with luck, have their aim spoiled by the need to take evasive action. Sergeant Horatio Chandler of 610 Squadron was performing the lonely task of aerodrome guard over Biggin Hill when a force of German fighters

Three Hurricanes are refuelled from a truck during the hectic fighting of the Battle of Britain. The pilots in flying dress stand nearby awaiting the call to return to combat.

came in low and fast to spray the airfield with bullets on a nuisance raid. Down dived Chandler. He managed to bounce a 109 from above and behind, shooting it out of the sky and causing it to crash beside the runway of Biggin Hill.

On 4 September Flying Officer Thomas Elsdon of 72 Squadron, flying out of Biggin Hill, took part in an attack on a German bomber force. On this occasion No.72 adopted the head-on approach. This gave them the advantage of approaching from a direction where the bombers could bring their main guns to bear, but meant that they had only a fleeting moment to fire, due to the high closing speed. This time the tactic was hugely successful. The leading aircraft fell victim to Elsdon's guns and the German formation broke up. Scattered and leaderless, the Germans made easy prey, with eight more going down to the guns of 72 Squadron.

Through all this defensive mayhem, Fighter Command were called upon to fly escort missions to protect the aircraft of RAF Bomber Command, that were flying over to the continent to try to destroy the gathering German invasion fleet. In ports from Normandy to Denmark craft of all types were being brought together to act as troop transports to carry the German army over the Channel.

Such combats mirrored those taking place over Kent, but this time in reverse. It was the British fighters that had to stick close to their bombers and the German fighters that could choose the time and place to attack. On one such mission, Wing Commander John Gillan was leading 615 Squadron as escort to a force of Blenheim IV bombers when the formation was bounced by German fighters over the Channel. Gillan led his squadron's Hurricanes to meet the threat, bringing down one 109 and seriously damaging another before the Germans withdrew.

These cross-Channel raids by Bomber Command received much less publicity than did the defensive exploits of Fighter Command over Britain. They were nonetheless vital. By mid-September they had succeeded in sinking eleven per cent of the gathering German invasion fleet.

On 2 September the pilots of 66 Squadron, then at Gravesend, were asked if they would volunteer for a secret mission to start at dawn the next day. Among the hands that went up was that of Hubert Allen, then a pilot officer, but later to be a wing commander and noted writer on air subjects. He and the two comrades selected were told nothing except that they were to be ready to take off at dawn the next day and would be led by Squadron Leader Oxspring.

At dawn, the puzzled pilots found Oxspring on the runway together with an Avro Anson, an elderly twin-engined type of reconnaissance aircraft. Oxspring's instructions were simple: the Spitfire pilots were to follow him and keep Jerry off his back. The four aircraft climbed into the sky and headed south. It transpired that the British army had decided to try shelling the invasion ships moored in Calais harbour with long range artillery. The crew of the Anson were to 'spot' for the guns, radioing back instructions on where to aim for maximum damage.

At just 10,000 ft the British aircraft circled Calais warily. The British guns opened up, sending shells splashing around their targets. Suddenly a large group of 109s was seen approaching fast. The Anson bolted home at maximum speed while Allen and his men fought a delaying action, before following in the race for Kent. The experiment was not repeated.

Another preparation to meet the expected invasion was kept top secret at the time. This was the construction of secret underground tunnels into RAF bases from nearby woodland. The location – and even the existence – of these tunnels was known to only a tiny number of local men. The idea was that if the Germans invaded they would undoubtedly take over the Kent RAF bases for the Luftwaffe. The local men would then sneak inside the bases through the tunnels on sabotage missions.

On the opposite side of the Channel, Goering and the Luftwaffe had problems of their own. The plan for the invasion of Britain called for Fighter Command to have been destroyed by the second week of September. Goering had hoped to achieve this by the end of August, but quite clearly had failed to do so. Meanwhile, the naval chiefs were pushing back the date by which they would be ready to carry the invasion army over the Channel. They now thought that the end of September was the most likely, though that was dangerously late in the season for a venture that relied on good weather and calm seas.

On 3 September, Goering assembled his senior commanders at The Hague for a conference to discuss the situation. Many in the Luftwaffe believed that the Kriegsmarine, the German navy, did not really intend to launch an invasion of Britain at all. There had been heavy naval losses in the Norwegian campaign and there were suspicions that the high command of the Kriegsmarine had no wish to take on the Royal Navy in the sort of open battle that would inevitably take place if the invasion went ahead. They thought the delay was merely a ruse to put off the invasion until winter weather closed in. Some even suspected that the navy

was hoping to lay the blame for the failure to invade Britain on the shoulders of the Luftwaffe.

If the invasion was not going to take place for at least a month, and perhaps not until the spring of 1941, the destruction of Fighter Command would no longer be an urgent imperative for the Luftwaffe. Desirable as the crushing of an enemy force might be, it was only worth doing if it helped to secure victory. So the debate now turned to how best to defeat Britain.

Hugo Sperrle, commander of Luftflotte 3, had long argued that the invasion of Britain would be a costly and risky enterprise. He maintained that Britain could best be defeated by starving the island nation of food and industrial supplies. He advocated returning the Luftwaffe to the bombing of docks, harbours and convoys in coastal waters, while the Kriegsmarine concentrated on attacking convoys on the high seas. Estimates vary, but if the Third Reich had devoted its massive industrial output to building U-boats and bombers it is likely that Britain would have been starved into surrender by late 1941 or early 1942.

However Goering knew, as Sperrle and the others did not, that this was never going to happen. Hitler believed that Britain had been reduced to insignificance and that the British would seek surrender terms sometime that winter – and he told anyone who would listen that he was prepared to be generous. Instead of concentrating on Britain, Hitler was already planning the invasion of Russia. On 2 September Hitler had ordered his general staff to start drawing up detailed plans for the conquest of Russia and to test them out in war games, which had to be completed by the end of November. Exactly when Hitler took the decision to invade Russia is unclear, but certainly by September 1940 the industrial might of the Third Reich was being turned to the manufacture of panzers and artillery, not U-boats and bombers.

If Britain were to be defeated, it was no use looking to starvation as anything other than an additional pressure when trying to find a diplomatic solution. Yet Goering was touchy about being blamed for the cancellation of the invasion of Britain. He was looking for a way to demonstrate that his beloved Luftwaffe had not only done its best, but had achieved significant results.

This was why he listened to the arguments of Albert Kesselring, commander of Luftflotte 2. Kesselring argued that if the invasion were not to take place, then the best use of the Luftwaffe over the winter would be

The shattered tail of a Heinkel 111 bomber stands beside bomb-blasted suburban homes.

to bomb London and other industrial cities. This would, Kesselring said, have the dual purpose of grinding down British industrial output, and thus reducing the nation's ability to wage war. At the same time the disruption to ordinary civilian life and the growing number of civilian deaths would pile pressure on the British government to accept Hitler's offer of a negotiated peace.

Knowing what he did, Goering supported Kesselring. The new style of attack would begin on 7 September, the target would be London.

The discussion then moved on to tactics. It was decided that there should now be two fighter escorts for each bomber formation. The first would fly alongside the bombers at a distance of about 250 yards to drive off any small formations of British fighters that got too close. A second escort would fly about 10,000 ft above the bombers to pounce down on any large bodies of British fighters seen to be approaching. The Germans were puzzled by the various British tactics of single squadron attacks alternating with big wing attacks, but the new tactic was designed to deal with both.

Just after lunchtime on 7 September, Goering and Kesselring stood on the cliffs near Calais to watch over 1,000 aircraft roar overhead on their way to London. Park was not expecting the change in German target, so

London burns. The dropping of incendiary bombs set off massive blazes in the docklands where warehouses went up in flames.

Residents of a suburban street collect their remaining belongings to be taken away after their homes have been made uninhabitable by bombs. Thousands of families were bombed out by the Luftwaffe during 1940.

his fighters were late on the scene. The East End of London was plastered with bombs. Over 300 people were killed, 2,000 wounded and large areas of the docks and warehouses destroyed. That night the bombers of Luftflotte 3 came over, bombing the fires still burning from earlier. The Germans came back on 10, 11, 13, 14 and 15 September to continue the bombing of London.

It was on 13 September that one of the most famous exploits by a man from Fighter Command, Kent, took place. Yorkshireman Sergeant James Lacey of 501 Squadron was widely known as 'Ginger' after a character in the popular Biggles books. He had joined the RAF on the outbreak of war and fought in France, where he used his Hurricane to shoot down five German aircraft. This was the Sergeant Lacey whose lost medal recommendation had been taken up by Dowding the previous month.

He had already come to the attention of the Press on 30 August 1940 when a film crew was visiting his base at Gravesend. The squadron was scrambled to meet a force of 50 Heinkel 111 bombers, plus a fighter escort, that was coming up the Thames from the North Sea. The movie crew filmed the squadron take off, then waited for them to come back.

In the air Lacey joined the attack on the Germans, but almost at once his engine oil line was severed by a bullet and black oil sprayed over his cockpit. Unable to see, Lacey inadvertently wandered into the German formation and came under heavy and sustained crossfire from the German gunners. His engine stopped as he threw back the cockpit canopy and stuck his head out to see where he was going. Preferring not to parachute down into the Thames estuary, Lacey put his stricken aircraft into a glide and headed for land. Amazingly he managed to nurse his Hurricane back to Gravesend, landing without power in front of the lenses of the filmcrew.

Lacey and his Hurricane, riddled by no fewer than 87 bullet holes, was splashed over the newsreels that week and featured in more than one newspaper.

On 13 September, Lacey and 501 Squadron went up to tackle a force of German bombers that had got through the front line of squadrons and were now over central London. Lacey spotted a lone Heinkel 111 at low altitude and went down after it. As he watched, Lacey saw the German unload its bombs onto Buckingham Palace. Seconds later, Lacey caught up with the German and opened fire. He saw his bullets strike home, but the bomber then dodged into a cloud.

The statue of Air Chief Marshal Sir Charles Portal that stands outside the Ministry of Defence in London. Portal was head of the RAF from 1940 to 1945.

An ambulance driver takes a break to stare at the German bombers during a daylight raid on London in September 1940. By this stage of the war women were filling many posts in the emergency services.

Lacey followed the fleeing German, emerging from the cloud to find himself almost on top of it. The German opened fire first, setting Lacey's engine on fire. Undeterred, Lacey returned fire and in turn set the German's engines ablaze. With both aircraft clearly doomed, all concerned took to their parachutes. Lacey escaped with minor burns, while one of the Germans was killed.

Lacey was commissioned as an officer in January 1941 and then became an instructor. In 1943 he was the test pilot who helped with the

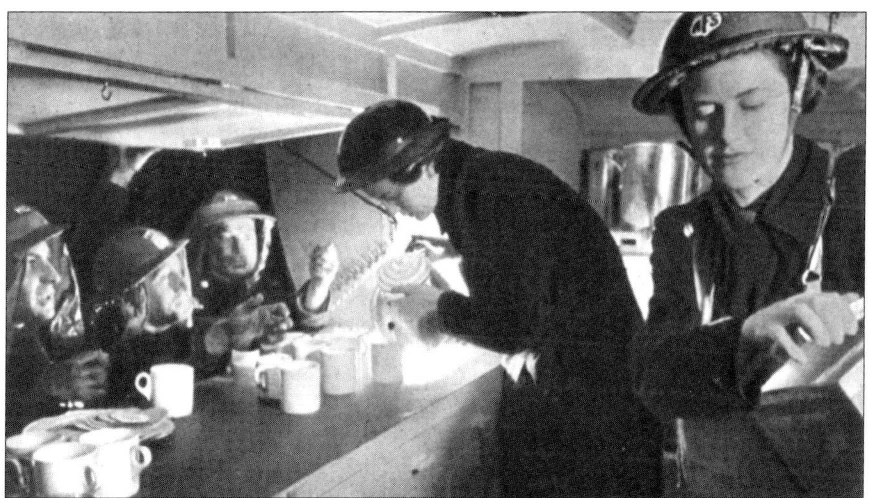

A group of firemen crowd round a mobile tea canteen in London, September 1940. As German raids on the capital reached a climax the firemen had to eat and drink when they could.

conversion of the Hurricane into a ground-attack aircraft when it was fitted with light bombs and tank-busting rockets. In 1943 he returned to combat, but this time far from Kent. He went to Burma to lead 17 Squadron, a Spitfire unit fighting Japanese aircraft over the inhospitable jungles of the Far East. He remained in the RAF after the war. His last day was marked by a massed flypast by Lightning jet fighters as he left his last base at RAF Topcliffe in 1967.

Meanwhile, Dowding had realised by the 16 September that the change in German strategy was definitive and ordered Park and Leigh-Mallory to alter their tactics to guard the cities, not the airfields. Dowding also began to wonder if the invasion had been cancelled. In fact it was on 17 September that Hitler formally made the decision to postpone the invasion of Britain, Operation Sealion, until the spring of 1941.

As soon as the invasion was off, Goering withdrew most of his Messerschmitt 110 fighters from the battle. They were converted to carry bombs so that they became fast-moving, high altitude bombers able to drop bombs reasonably accurately and get away again before the British fighters could climb to attack them. They would not return to action for some weeks.

Dornier Do17

Type:	five crew medium bomber
Engine:	2 x 1000 hp Bramo Fafnir 323P
Wingspan:	59 ft
Length:	51 ft 9 in
Height:	14 ft 11 in
Weight:	Empty 13,145 lb
	Loaded 18,937 lb
Armament:	6 x 7.9 mm machine guns in various positions
Bombload:	2205 lb
Max speed:	263 mph
Ceiling:	26,740 ft
Range:	720 miles
Production:	1200

Dornier's Do17 range of bombers began in 1934 when Lufthansa rejected a Dornier design for a fast mail plane. By late 1935 Dornier had converted the prototype to a bomber with an internal bomb bay, machine-gun mountings and a glazed nose. This entered Luftwaffe service in 1938 as the Do17M, a bomber, and the Do17P, a long range reconnaissance scout. It quickly acquired the nickname of 'Flying Pencil', due to its thin fuselage. Experience in the Spanish Civil War highlighted problems with the bomber version, which by 1938 was replaced by the Do17Z, to which the figures given here apply. This had a much-enlarged front section of fuselage to house extra guns and other equipment. An export version was produced for Germany's allies, such as Hungary, but by 1942 the Luftwaffe was phasing the Do17 out of front-line service.

Luftflotte 3 was by this time settling into the role of skillful night bombing of cities. About 300 bombers were sent over each night, with about half of them going to bomb London. Luftflotte 2 continued to be used during daylight hours. Heavy fighter escorts accompanied the bombers as they pounded towns and cities near the coast, as well as London.

Messerschmitt Bf 110

Type:	Two seat long-range fighter
Engine:	2 x 1100hp Daimler-Benz DB601A
Wingspan:	53 ft 4 in
Length:	39 ft 8 in
Height:	11 ft 6 in
Weight:	Empty 9920 lb
	Loaded 15,300 lb
Armament:	2 x 20 mm cannon and 4 x 7.9 mm machine guns in nose plus 1 x 7.9 mm machine gun in rear cockpit
Max speed:	349 mph
Ceiling:	32,000 ft
Range:	565 miles
Production:	6050

Before the war began the Luftwaffe, unlike some other air forces, had worried that their bombers might not be able to fend off attacks by fighters. The need for an escort fighter with a similar range to the bombers was recognised, but the additional fuel tanks would make the resulting aircraft heavy. The answer, the Germans thought, was to provide twin engines and a heavy armament to give increased speed and hitting power to make up for a lack of nimbleness. The Bf110 entered service in July 1938 and by the time of the Battle of Britain was available in no fewer than seven variants, mostly concerned with armament or increased range. The figures given above are for the C5 model. After its lack of success against the Spitfire and Hurricane, the 110 was redesigned to be either a fast bomber or a night-fighter in a further 20 variants. It remained in production until the end of 1944.

Chapter 6

A New Commander

The change of German tactics from daylight raids on airfields and aircraft factories to mixed day and night raids on cities and towns was both a relief and a worry for Dowding and the higher ranks at Fighter Command.

On the plus side, the change gave Fighter Command a much-needed break. The constant pounding of airbases, especially in Kent, had caused heavy casualties among highly trained groundcrew, who could not easily be replaced, and had severely disrupted the smooth efficiency of the command. Now that the bases were no longer being bombed – or at least not so heavily nor so often – the fighter squadrons could return to a higher level of efficiency. Certainly the pilots appreciated knowing that at the end of an arduous mission they stood a good chance of being able to land back at base rather than finding it a smoking ruin.

Hugh Eliot who flew out of Manston in 1940. He was later to be killed in action in 1945.

One of the activities that the Command was able to catch up with was the award of medals. Throughout the Battle of Britain feats of outstanding skill or bravery had resulted in recommendations, and in most cases awards, of immediate medals. Now that the pressure was off, however, time was found to reward the less spectacular but no less heroic feats of sustained work and devotion to duty.

Pilot Officer Keith Gillman of 32 Squadron, who flew out of Biggin Hill during the Battle of Britain. This official photo was widely used during the war and came to symbolise the pilots of Fighter Command. (Manston S&H Mem)

In October 1940 Pilot Officer Anthony Bartley of 92 Squadron was awarded the Distinguished Flying Cross. During the hectic months he had shot down no fewer than eight German aircraft and, as his squadron commander wrote, 'has always displayed great coolness in action and proved himself a clever and determined fighter'. Flight Lieutenant George Christie was likewise awarded a DFC, having shot down seven German aircraft and 'shown outstanding ability and leadership over a long period of air operations'.

Sergeant Reggie Llewellyn of 213 Squadron, being an NCO, was awarded the Distinguished Flying Medal. By October his score had reached four Ju88s, four Me110s, three Me109s, one Heinkel 111 destroyed, plus several probables. 'He has,' wrote his commander when making the recommendation for a medal 'at all times shown great courage and devotion to duty.'

The main problem for Dowding was that the bombing of cities was leading to rapidly escalating civilian casualties. Not only was this a real

Pilots of a Spitfire squadron study a map. The photo was taken for a Post Office Savings drive and was possibly taken in Kent. (Manston S&H Mem)

The central control room of the Observer Corps. The staff below received reports from Observer Corps outposts and marked the position of all enemy aircraft on the table map. The staff on the balcony above reported those movements to Fighter Command HQ.

concern in itself, but it led to questions being asked by politicians whose constituents were now being killed by the Luftwaffe. Not since the French had demanded that fighter squadrons be sent to France had Dowding come under such sustained outside pressure.

The political problems were made all the worse by the fact that the Germans were now flying increasingly at night. In the pre-war period air staff on all sides had assumed that, as in the First World War, all air fighting would take place in daylight hours. It was thought that bombers with defensive armament or fighter escort could get through to their targets in considerable numbers and inflict worthwhile amounts of damage. The Battle of Britain had shown that this was the case only over short ranges. When bombing targets in support of the ground army, the Luftwaffe had been able to get in and out again without serious loss. But when attacking targets at any distance from their base, bomber losses mounted alarmingly. This was why Goering was now only attacking inland cities and targets at night.

Because the RAF had assumed that bombing would take place only in daylight hours, it had designed its defences accordingly. The radar system and ground-based radio controllers could accurately direct fighter squadrons to get them into a position to attack enemy bombers, but the fighter pilots needed to be able to see the German aircraft in order to aim their guns. At night they could often not see their hands in front of their faces, so the Germans were raiding virtually unopposed. It had been assumed that searchlights would illuminate any enemy raiders for fighters to shoot at. In the event there proved to be too many raiders and not enough searchlights for this to be a realistic option. Some bombers were shot down at night, but not many.

The fact that the Germans could not see much better to aim their bombs was little consolation as bombs aimed at an aircraft factory and missing would hit the houses nearby. The situation would get very much worse in November, when Goering ordered a halt to nearly all daylight raids. The long winter nights became alive with German bombers over Britain.

The answer, as Dowding had recognised some months earlier, was to fit a radar set into a fighter. This would allow the pilot to aim his guns at the blip on the radar screen, which he could see, rather than at the enemy aircraft, which he could not. The first air-to-air radar system was ready for testing in the spring of 1940. It proved to be so heavy that only a bomber could carry it, and in any case it was unreliable. Dowding was promised a

A pair of Dornier Do17Z bombers over London in September 1940, as shown in a German photo released to the press at the time. (Manston S&H Mem)

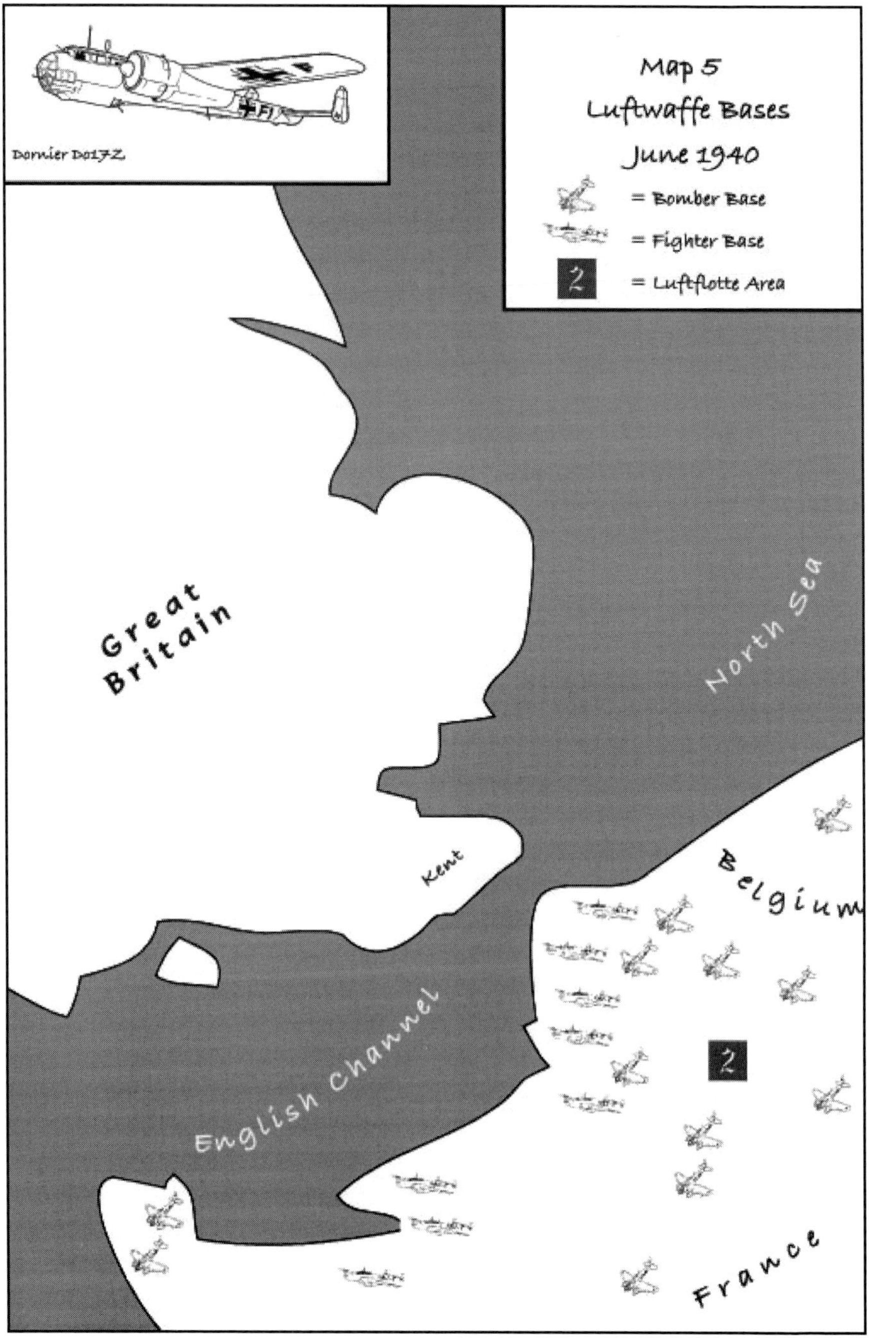

Dornier Do17Z
Map 5
Luftwaffe Bases
June 1940
= Bomber Base
= Fighter Base
2 = Luftflotte Area
Great Britain
North Sea
Kent
Belgium
English Channel
2
France

reliable set by the autumn and that it would be small and light enough to fit into the new twin-engined Beaufighter that was then entering production.

Meanwhile, Fighter Command's pilots had to get by as best they could. They performed best on moonlit nights, when they stood a chance of seeing the enemy, and it soon became clear that two pairs of eyes were better than one. The old Defiants with their gun turret were brought back into the fray and achieved some success.

Not all German raids took place at night. One raid that was heading for a coastal target in October consisted of a large force of Dornier 17 bombers escorted by fighters. The first RAF squadron to encounter the force drove off the fighters, so when 66 Squadron arrived a few minutes later the Dorniers were unescorted. Pilot Officer Crelin Bodie was among the pilots to attack. The first pass caused the Germans to break formation.

Bodie was then able to dive down on a lone Dornier. A single burst from his guns caused the aircraft to explode in a massive ball of flame. Bodie then found himself alone in the sky, his squadron comrades having gone off in search of prey. Hoping to find them above the blanket of cloud, Bodie climbed. As he emerged from the top of the cloud into bright sunlight he found himself almost immediately underneath two more Dorniers. He opened fire on one, which quickly went into a dive with smoke pouring from an engine. Turning to the remaining bomber, Bodie faced more of a challenge. His prey twisted and turned to avoid his attacks, the gunners firing back at him whenever he got within range. The chase went on for some minutes, but eventually Bodie inflicted crucial damage on the German. As the bomber went down into the cloud, Bodie followed it and came out underneath the murk in time to see the German hit the sea with a great splash. It was his sixth kill since he joined the squadron four weeks earlier.

Flight Lieutenant Denys Gillam had an equally adventurous day attacking German formations raiding coastal targets. He took off in his Hurricane and got engaged in a dogfight with a number of Messerschmitt 110s. He shot one down, but was immediately caught by another German fighter and saw his own engine shudder as it was hit by cannon shells and then caught fire. Gillam leapt from his cockpit and floated down to earth to land only a couple of miles from his base. Discarding his parachute he walked back.

Barely had Gillam arrived at the airfield when the alarm was sounded again. Leaping into another Hurricane, Gillam climbed for height, shot

The burning wreckage of a Dornier Do17z bomber brought down over Kent in August 1940. (Manston S&H Mem)

down a Junkers 88 and returned to base, landing less than eleven minutes after having taken off.

No less demanding were the exploits of Pilot Officer Kenneth MacKenzie of 501 Squadron. On patrol off Dover later in October, MacKenzie sighted a formation of eight 109s below him. He dived down to deliver a high-speed passing attack and then swept on. One of the German fighters was damaged and went down to sea level as it turned towards France. Unwilling to let his prey escape, MacKenzie went down after it. But when he pushed the gun button, nothing happened. His guns had failed.

Still determined to destroy his enemy, despite his lack of guns, MacKenzie flew alongside the Messerschmitt and used his wingtip to nudge the enemy aircraft. The second prod was enough to break the Messerschmitt's tail plane and send it cartwheeling into the sea.

The pilots of the other 109s had meanwhile seen what was going on and dived down to take their revenge on MacKenzie. The British pilot weaved desperately, but finally a stream of bullets smashed into his aircraft. Streaming smoke and glycol, MacKenzie nursed his stricken aircraft over the coast, and then flopped it down into a crash-landing in a field. Amazingly, he walked away without a scratch.

Also mercifully uninjured was Wing Commander Stanley Vincent. In October this senior officer was in the air to observe British fighter tactics against the Germans. The formation he was meant to be observing attacked 15 Dorniers with a large Messerschmitt escort. Vincent himself joined in the action and downed a Messerschmitt 109. He thus became a unique pilot in the world, being the only fighter pilot to shoot down an enemy aircraft in both the First and Second World Wars.

A Luftwaffe publicity photo from October 1940 shows a Heinkel III bomber over London.

In November, Goering ordered that air attacks on Britain should concentrate on the night bombing of industrial cities. By flying at night the bombers could afford to fly lower and more slowly than during the day, when they were vulnerable to fighters. This meant that they could carry heavier bomb loads to more distant targets. Targeting industrial cities meant that the bombs dropped should hit something that would damage the British war effort, even though bombing at night was usually fairly inaccurate.

To cure the accuracy problem the Germans developed a navigational aid known as the X-gerat. This involved the transmission of four narrow, high power radio beams across Britain from stations in occupied Europe. The first beam was directed straight over the target. The bombers would fly out to intersect this beam some distance from the target, then turn along it. A second beam cut across the first, about 30 miles from the target, to alert the navigator that the aircraft was approaching its objective. The third beam was met twelve miles from the target and the fourth three miles. By timing the gap between the final two beams, the navigator on board could calculate the aircraft's speed and so decide when to drop the bombs from the aircraft's altitude.

Assuming that all went well, German bombers could reliably get their bombs to within some 400 yards of any chosen spot in Britain. The only real problem from the German viewpoint was that the narrowness of the main beam meant that only one or two bombers could fly along it at a time without a danger of collision in the dark. The result was a steady stream of bombers rather than a single massed raid.

The first time the new bombing technique was tried out was on 14 November 1940 in an operation code-named Moonlight Sonata. Through listening to Luftwaffe radio traffic in the days beforehand, the British code breakers learned that a major raid using a new navigational device was due, but did not know either the target or what the device was. As a result the German bombers got through unopposed. Some 450 bombers rained down 500 tons of explosive bombs, plus nearly 1,000 incendiaries. The centre of Coventry was completely destroyed, 500 people died and 1,200 were seriously wounded.

The next day, a daylight raid was organised by the Germans, aiming at various targets in Kent. This time the intruders were the nimble Messerschmitt 109s, but adapted to carry bombs. This was the E4B, an experimental version of the 109 that proved to be so successful that it was

Communal canteens were set up to serve emergency food to civilians who had either been bombed out of their homes or were unable to get home owing to disruption caused by the bombing.

The famous church of St Clement Danes in London's Fleet Street goes up in flames. Designed by Sir Christopher Wren to replace a medieval church destroyed in the Great Fire of 1665, St Clement's was gutted by this fire started by incendiary bombs. It was subsequently rebuilt and now serves as the home church of the RAF.

developed into the F1 fighter-bomber variant. They were designed to fly fast, dropping their bombs on any useful target that offered itself. If they met RAF fighters, they would drop their heavy bombs and instantly become nimble, fast fighters well able to hold their own. On this occasion 50 of the new 109s came up the Thames estuary, and 92 Squadron was sent up from Biggin Hill to meet them. Among the British pilots was Sergeant Don Kingaby, who already had ten German aircraft shot down to his credit.

The Germans were at 17,000 ft when the Spitfires got on their tails. The Germans dropped their bombs and turned to fight. Kingaby pounced on a 109, fired two short bursts and sent it spinning down to crash near Gravesend. The rest of the Germans fled and No.92 landed in time for lunch.

That afternoon the squadron was scrambled again, but this time they were met over Selsey Bill by a force of 109s that outnumbered them by 3:1. The Germans had the advantage of height and dived to attack. After a confused swirl of combat, Kingaby found himself above and behind three 109s that were making off south towards France. The last of the Germans appeared damaged. Kingaby dived, fired a short burst and saw the straggler burst into flames and dive into the sea.

The return fire from German bombers could be destructive, as shown by the battered state of this Hurricane's tail.

The other German pilots had seen neither Kingaby's attack nor their comrade's destruction and carried on as if nothing had happened. Kingaby dived, then came up from behind and underneath the leading German. He fired one long burst that seemed to have no effect, then a second short burst, at which the German aircraft exploded. Kingaby guessed that he must still have had his bomb on board so savage was the blast. There was nothing left of the aircraft but fragments of debris falling down.

Kingaby assumed the other Messerschmitt would by this time have fled at high speed for France, and was surprised to see it coming round to attack him. There followed several minutes of jockeying for position as the fighters looped and swooped around the sky, then Kingaby got in a burst that sent the German down into the sea.

Four enemy fighters for one pilot in a single day was a record for Biggin Hill. Kingaby was later sent off to London to describe the events in a broadcast for the BBC, while his score was added to that of 92 Squadron. It was while doing the necessary paperwork that a clerk realised that pilots flying out of Biggin Hill during the war had downed over 590 German aircraft. By 29 November the total stood at 599. No other RAF Fighter Command station could boast a figure even approaching this. Speculation was rife as to who would get the 600th kill, and when.

The next day, 30 November, dawned grey and dull. Heavy mist blanketed the ground and solid cloud cover was at less than 1,000 ft. All aircraft were grounded. Deprived of their anticipated success, the pilots, ground crew and admin staff of Biggin Hill sloped off to take care of their various routine jobs. Suddenly the throaty roar of Spitfire engines shattered the peace and two fighters raced down the runway to take to the air. 'Of all the bloody cheek,' exclaimed the station commander.

It turned out that the two pilots were Mungo-Park and Stephens, the two flight leaders of 92 Squadron. Instantly the operations room was packed and all doors blocked by eager listeners as the pilot's radio conversation came over the loudspeakers. With rather exaggerated casualness, Mungo-Park called in to report that they were on a 'voluntary patrol' – in other words disobeying orders. The Biggin Hill controller phoned 11 Group HQ to ask for advice. 'Send those two idiots to Deal,' came the reply. 'There is a convoy off the coast that might tempt Jerry even in this muck.'

Several minutes passed as the two Spitfires circled over Deal. Then came the news that a small German formation was approaching at 30,000 ft

A much reproduced photo of a crashed Dornier Do17Z bomber in an English field. The original caption proclaimed 'The RAF Joins the Harvest'. (Manston S&H Mem)

from the south. Mungo-Park and Stephens were directed in a sweeping arc that would bring them up behind the Germans, which turned out to be a force of eight 109s. 'Tally-ho,' called out Stephens over his radio when he caught sight of the Germans. The two Spitfires came up carefully from below to pick off the rearmost German. Stephens fired first, but missed, so Mungo-Park let fly and saw fragments flying off the German aircraft. Then Stephens came back and fired a long burst from a range of barely 20 yards. The German fighter lurched, then dived. The pilot was seen to scramble out and take to his parachute as the doomed fighter disappeared into the solid cloud cover below.

Back at Biggin Hill the waiting staff erupted in cheers and everyone made a dash for the bar. Stephens and Mungo-Park landed a short while later and, after taking the time to write out hurried reports, raced to join the celebrations. The pilot of the doomed Messerschmitt was not so lucky. Oberleutnant Schmidt came to ground safely near Dungeness and was

Groundcrew rearm a Spitfire in August 1940. The thin elliptical wing of the Spitfire made this job a fiddly operation for the men.

picked up by the Home Guard. He was, however, seriously wounded by a bullet from one of the Spitfires and despite being taken to hospital died the next day.

Meanwhile, the problems within Fighter Command's higher echelons were reaching crisis point. Freed from the immediate pressures of battle, Leigh-Mallory and Park had revived their disagreements over big wings. Memos and letters were going back and forth, trying to rake over previous events and to apportion blame for when things had gone wrong. Dowding, who by now was wrestling with the night-fighter problem, thought the issue academic, since the Germans were no longer coming over in large daylight formations, and tried to close the dispute down.

However, Leigh-Mallory's behind-the-scenes campaign with politicians and Air Ministry officials ensured that the dispute would not go away, and indeed was taken to higher authorities. The disputes that followed were complex and tortuous and remained the subject of heated argument in RAF circles for years.

Dowding had been due to leave Fighter Command in the spring of 1940, but had stayed on due to the sudden threat from the Luftwaffe. Now that the immediate threat of invasion had gone, the opportunity was taken to move Dowding on, giving his replacement time to settle in before the good spring weather revived the threat. It was unfortunate, to say the least, that the politicians chose to oust Dowding when he was embroiled in an internal dispute of some acrimony. The impression was given that he was being booted out in disgrace, rather than moved on in a normal way, and many senior officers never forgave Leigh-Mallory for his actions.

The fact the Dowding did not receive a promotion to Marshal of the Royal Air Force, as would have been usual, spawned the impression that he was being treated poorly. The impression was reinforced when Dowding later retired from the RAF altogether. Other senior commanders with a victory such as the Battle of Britain to their credit were given a seat in the House of Lords. Dowding was not.

Dowding was not the only senior commander to be replaced in November. Park, commander of 11 Group that included Kent, was also moved on. He went to Malta, where he organised the air defence of that besieged island with his customary skill and courage. It was, perhaps, tactless that Park should be replaced by none other than Leigh-Mallory. Dowding's position as head of Fighter Command was taken by William Sholto Douglas, a senior RAF officer with an outstanding career, who had most recently been serving at the Air Ministry.

Douglas was fortunate in that his arrival at Bentley Priory coincided with the arrival at front-line squadrons of the heavily armed Beaufighter equipped with air-to-air radar, known at the time as AI. On the night of 19 November a Beaufighter from 604 Squadron in the West Country brought down a Junkers Ju88. It was the first radar kill of the war. The pilot, John Cunningham, later became famous as 'Cat's Eyes' Cunningham, with nineteen victims shot down by AI. The story was put about that his phenomenal success was due to his eating large quantities of carrots to help him see in the dark. All mention of AI was strictly forbidden in an attempt to stop the Germans discovering its existence.

It would take some time for the night-fighter force to increase in strength; there were only six such squadrons by January 1941. The AI sets were expensive and slow to produce, while the training needed to operate them was long and involved.

The Beaufighter was not the only new aircraft entering service at this time. In December Biggin Hill greeted the arrival of an uprated Spitfire,

the MkV. It looked much the same as the old Mk1, but this MkV packed a powerful punch in the shape of two 20 mm cannons as well as four machine guns. Less obvious was a new type of carburettor in the engine, which solved the one 'bug' in the Mk1, its tendency to misfire when in a steep dive, as the carburettor relied on gravity to feed fuel into the cylinder block.

This first MkV was the only one in service, so it was with some trepidation that Flight Lieutenant 'Pancho' Villa learned that he was to take it into action for the first time. There had been much debate in Fighter Command circles about how the new cannon would work in practice. Everyone knew of the devastating effects of cannon shell strikes after being on the receiving end of the 20 mm cannon in the German fighters. What was not so clear was whether or not the added hitting power made up for the slower rate of fire and smaller number of rounds that could be carried in the aircraft.

The answer came in dramatic fashion when, after some incident free patrols, Villa met a 109 off South Foreland. He dived to attack, alerting his base over the radio to his actions. He switched his radio back on to announce 'opening fire'. The next thing the startled control room staff at Biggin Hill heard was Villa's excited voice, 'Christ Almighty. The bugger's blown up. Blown to pieces, do you hear me? Into bloody little pieces.'

The debate over the merits of the cannon was over. The MkV was to become the most numerous of all the various types of Spitfire produced during the war, with 6,472 entering service.

On 20 December 1940 Fighter Command went on the offensive for the first time. Two Spitfires of 66 Squadron of 11 Group, piloted by Flight Lieutenant George Christie and Pilot Officer Crelin Bodie took off in the morning. They flew across the Channel at wavetop height and headed for the Luftwaffe base at Le Touquet, which lay very close to the French coast. The Spitfires roared across the airfield, spraying bullets around at random, then came back the way they had come before the startled Germans could respond.

Although the damage inflicted was slight, and at the time nobody in Fighter Command knew if any damage had been done at all, the mission was counted a success. The idea of two fighters dashing over the Channel, shooting up a ground target and racing home again was dubbed a 'rhubarb'. Douglas gave permission for group headquarters to sanction or not any suggestion for a rhubarb that came up from a squadron. The only

Bristol Beaufighter

Type:	Twin seat night-fighter
Engine:	2 x 1400 Bristol Hercules III
Wingspan:	57 ft 10 in
Length:	41 ft 4 in
Height:	15 ft 10 in
Weight:	Empty 14,069 lb
	Loaded 21,100 lb
Armament:	4 x 20 mm cannon in nose plus 6 x .303 machine guns in wings
Max speed:	323 mph
Ceiling:	28,900 ft
Range:	1170 miles
Production:	5584

The superb Beaufighter grew out of the equally impressive Beaufort, a long-range bomber developed for Coastal Command that could carry a torpedo as an alternative to conventional bombs. It entered production late in 1939, the first aircraft reaching Fighter Command in October 1940. The concept was to have a fighter large enough to carry an air-to-air radar set and a second crew member to operate it. The designers assumed that there would be time for only a short burst of fire at a target, hence the heavy armament. The Beaufighter was later modified to be an anti-shipping strike aircraft able to carry either rockets or a torpedo in addition to its cannon. The unusually quiet engines of this aircraft caused it to be nicknamed 'whispering death' by the Japanese.

stipulation he made was that they could only be carried out on days when there was plenty of low cloud cover. The fighters had to be able to hide if they stumbled across a superior force of German fighters.

At last Fighter Command was hitting back. Before long, the fighter pilots of Kent would be hitting back on a much larger scale.

Chapter 7

Circus
Time

After the change of higher command within Fighter Command there was a rethinking of strategy. It was now clear that any German invasion of Britain could not take place until the good weather of spring arrived in April or May 1941. The head of Fighter Command, Sholto Douglas, was confident that with the increasing numbers of pilots and aircraft arriving under his command over the winter he would be able to stop the Germans gaining control of the air. Nevertheless a good deal of planning and preparation went on so that Fighter Command would be ready for the fray when it came.

Meanwhile, Douglas had to keep his men busy over the winter. He was as determined to keep his own men in training and ready for action as he was to probe continually and test the strength of the Luftwaffe across the Channel.

The attack on Le Touquet airfield by two Spitfires in December had shown the way forward. These low-level, high-speed missions by two or three fighters were dubbed 'rhubarbs'. A similar mission but carried out with an entire squadron was designated a 'rodeo'. While rhubarbs could be suggested by squadrons and approved by Group HQ, rodeos had to be authorised and planned by Fighter Command HQ. 'Jim Crows' were regular patrols that were carried out day after day along set routes to search for enemy activity. Most of them took place over the Channel.

A Bristol Beaufighter Mk1 flies over a snow-covered Britain. The introduction of this aircraft in March 1941 revolutionised the RAF's night-fighter effort.

Rather more formal, in that they had a definite objective, were 'ramrods'. These were bombing missions undertaken by the squadrons of RAF Bomber Command to which Fighter Command was expected to provide fighter cover. Most such missions had one force of fighters providing cover to the bombers on the way out, with a second force taking off later to escort them back when the first group of fighters began to run low on fuel.

Altogether different were the 'circus' missions. These were designed to appear to the Germans as if they were a normal ramrod, but in fact were structured so that it was Fighter Command who took the lead. The bombers were present only in small numbers and were there simply to give the illusion of a bombing mission. In fact the half a dozen or so bombers were escorted by as many as 50 or more fighters. The aim was to lure the German fighters up to attack the bombers, and then for the British fighters to pounce on them in overwhelming numbers.

The first circus took place on 9 January 1941, with the Luftwaffe airfield of Forêt de Guines as the ostensible target of the six Blenheim bombers. Escorting the Blenheims were three squadrons of Hurricanes. This was a

The briefing room of RAF Manston, prepared for briefing the pilots about an upcoming ramrod mission over occupied Europe. (RAF Manston Mus)

Two Spitfire squadrons set off for a circus operation over France. The second squadron is above and behind the first, to form an upper escort.

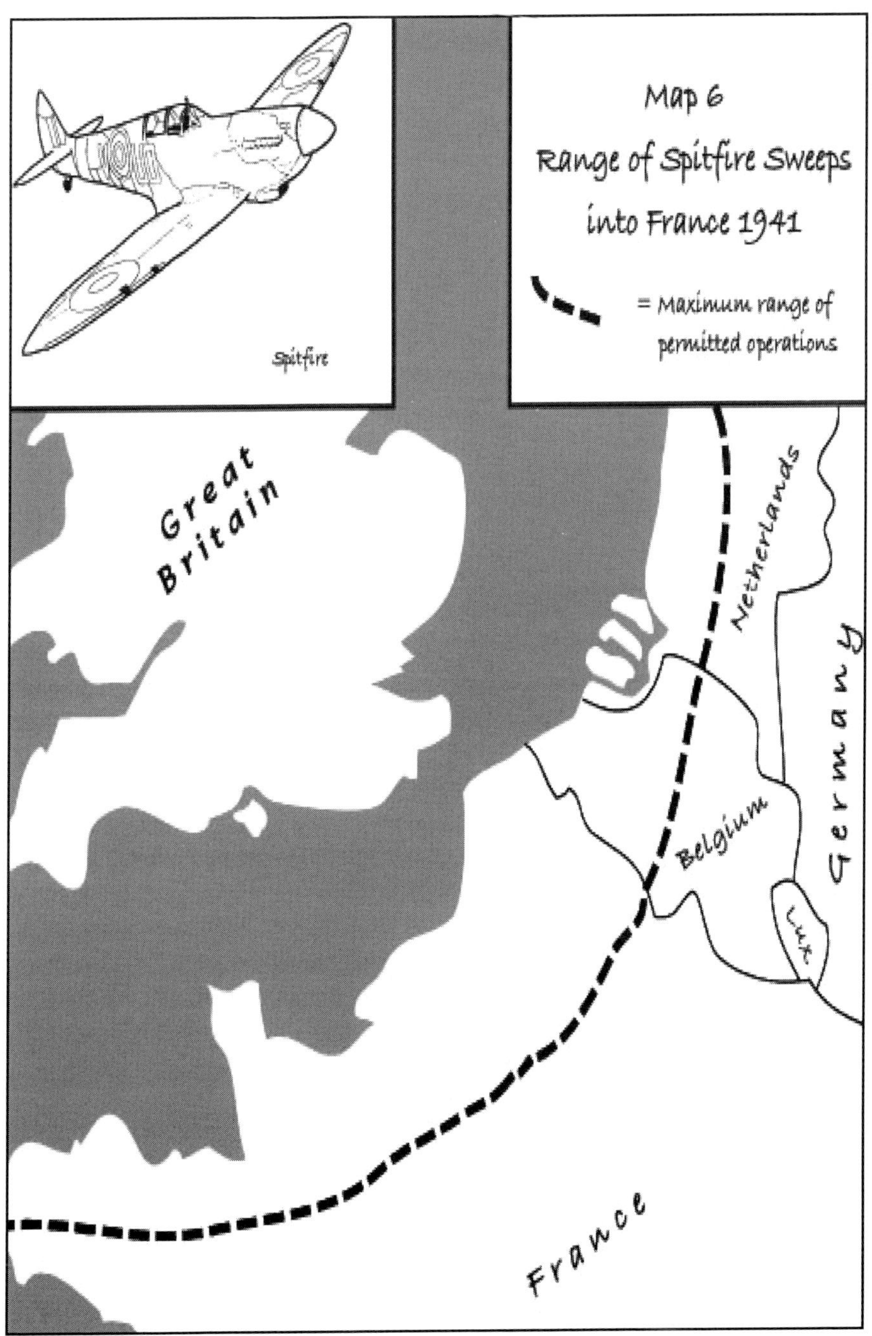
Spitfire
Map 6
Range of Spitfire Sweeps
into France 1941
= Maximum range of
permitted operations
Great Britain
Netherlands
Germany
Belgium
Lux
France

strong escort in itself, but the shock for the Germans was intended to be the three squadrons of Spitfires positioned several thousand feet higher up. None of these aircraft came from Kent, but the entire fighter force of Biggin Hill was on readiness to take off in case they were needed.

The circus got to its target without incident, apart from some flak, which caused no damage. The Blenheims dropped their bombs and turned for home. They were over the Channel when the squadron of Messerschmitt 109s sent up to attack caught up with them. By this time the British fighters were low on fuel. They beat off the attack, shooting down two Germans for the cost of one Hurricane, but were unable to engage in a massed dogfight as intended, since they needed to get home. As it was, one Spitfire ran out of fuel and crashlanded into a field. The Biggin Hill fighters were not called upon.

This first circus was judged a partial success, although a detailed study by intelligence officers after the event concluded that some new form of radio traffic was needed if six or more squadrons were to be coordinated accurately over enemy territory. Only later would it become clear that radar gave only approximately accurate readings for the position of squadrons once they were over France. This, as much as radio reception, would cause serious problems.

Meanwhile the business of defending Britain continued to take up most of Fighter Command's time. In January, 92 Squadron was sent up to intercept a formation of Germans heading up the Thames Estuary. Pilot Officer Anthony Bartley spotted a straggling Heinkel 111 and dived to the attack. He was so intent on the task in hand that it was not until he had sent the German crashing into the sea that Bartley realised he was flying at barely 150 ft over Southend Pier. The pier and seafront were crowded with daytrippers enthusiastically cheering the Spitfire in its combat. Bartley gave them a cheery wave and headed back to base at Manston.

Meanwhile, Fighter Command was being restructured along the lines long favoured by Leigh-Mallory, now commander of 11 Group. Instead of having individual squadrons based at airfields for tactical purposes, but being responsible directly to group, Leigh-Mallory favoured the creation of wings made up of several squadrons each. In general a wing would consist of three fighter squadrons, at least one of which had to be equipped with Spitfires. Each wing would be based at a particular airfield, where all support and administrative staff would work, though some

A squadron of Hurricane MkII fighters in flight. The MkII entered service in 1941 with an uprated engine and more effective armament of four 20 mm cannons. Not visible here are the two 500 lb bombs this version could carry under the wings. The MkII carved out a career as a ground-attack aircraft during 1941 and 1942.

aircraft might operate out of smaller nearby airfields. The wing would now be the basic tactical unit of Fighter Command.

Not that the Luftwaffe was allowing Fighter Command to set the pace entirely. Those fighters adapted to carry bombs were still launching their

hit-and-run raids at high speed. Manston, being near the coast, received more such raids than any other station. A particularly heavy raid in mid-February saw no fewer than 30 Messerschmitts come roaring in off the sea to bomb and strafe the base. In an attempt to ward off these raids the number of Jim Crow patrols was stepped up.

One particular exponent of the Jim Crow was Sergeant Paul Louis of 615 Squadron, who was to fly almost 100 of them in 1941, as well as 38 other missions. He ended the year being credited with a Ju88 destroyed and a 109 probable. It may not sound a high score, but targets were fewer to come by in 1941 than they had been in 1940. In their place came long, arduous hours of flying, never knowing when the Hun would pounce from the sun.

In theory the radar system should have identified enemy formations and their position, so allowing British fighters to avoid being surprised. Unfortunately, those controllers tasked with giving directions to fighter pilots in the air did not always have accurate information and, when they did, they were not always able to appreciate the complex three-dimensional situation in the air. As a result squadron commanders did not always fully trust the instructions they were given.

A typical example of what could go wrong occurred to 66 Squadron on 14 February 1941. The Spitfires had been scrambled to face an incoming daylight raid and were climbing for height beneath a solid layer of cloud at around 10,000 ft. The controller instructed the fighters to climb through the cloud, estimated to be 3,000 ft thick, and so emerge about ten miles from the enemy and in a position to climb above them before attacking.

What the controller had not appreciated was that when flying up through the cloud the Spitfire pilots would be surrounded by grey mist. When they emerged out of the cloud into bright sunlight they would be temporarily dazzled. And the situation was made worse by the fact that the Germans would be up sun of them.

When the Spitfires emerged from the cloud, the Germans spotted them at once and the fighter escort dived to the attack. Dazzled, the British pilots did not see the Germans coming until it was too late. Squadron Leader 'Dizzy' Allen got a bullet through his right arm as a fusillade of shots struck his aircraft. He pushed down in a dive to get into the safety of the cloud, then nursed his crippled aircraft back to Biggin Hill. On landing he found that his brakes had failed, so Allen ran into a bomb crater and had to be helped out of the cockpit by ground crew armed with sledgehammers. The Spitfire, it turned out, had been hit by 43 bullets and one explosive cannon shell. Allen was out of action for weeks.

During all this the task of dealing with the German night raids on British cities continued unabated. Over the winter months the strength and frequency of the bombing raids varied greatly with the weather, but they continued mercilessly. London was hit on 57 consecutive nights, each time with an average of 160 bombers.

At first the RAF's night-fighter effort continued much as it had done in late 1940. A few radar-equipped Beaufighters made impressive forays, but the bulk of the effort was made by conventional fighters relying on ground-based searchlights to illuminate raiders for them. Sergeant Alf Cumbers of 141 Squadron was a gunner in Defiants during this period. Together with his pilot, Flying Officer Waddington, he flew 42 missions in the first three months of 1941, shooting down one Heinkel 111 into the sea near Dover. Fred Gash was another successful air gunner on Defiants. Flying from Manston, he shot down a Heinkel 111 and damaged a second.

In March 1941, 264 Squadron with their Defiants came to Biggin Hill. At first they were tasked with trying out a new concept: firing their guns 'blind' following the instructions of highly accurate ground-based radar. Out of 76 flights there were only seven contacts and the fighters opened fire only four times. The problem proved to be that the new radar was of

A Hurricane night-fighter awaits take off. The only real adaptation to night-fighting was to paint the aircraft black so that the German air gunners would find it harder to locate the attacker.

A group of Hurricane pilots at rest in the officers' mess. The men are wearing 'night goggles', which enabled them to move around in lit rooms without spoiling their night vision. Thus when an enemy aircraft was located by radar they would be able to take off immediately to begin the difficult task of trying to spot it in the dark night sky.

such a short range that the German bombers had flown out of range by the time the fighters got close enough to open fire. The idea was abandoned.

Returning to their more conventional tactics of relying on moonlight, searchlights or luck, the Defiant crews began to add to their scores. Sergeant Fred Barker became the top-scoring air gunner of all time when he shot down his thirteenth victim over Godalming.

A searchlight in action in the autumn of 1941. By this date it was the anti-aircraft guns that mostly used searchlights to illuminate targets, as the night-fighters were increasingly equipped with air-to-air radar.

Pilot Eric Barwell and gunner Sergeant Martin of 264 were meanwhile not enjoying any luck at all. They had been flying night patrols for seven months without firing their guns – though they had seen a German once, back in October 1940. The night of 29 April would, however, prove to be eventful. The two men took off in their Defiant as radar reported German aircraft taking off from France. It was a brilliant moonlit night – ideal for night-fighters operating without airborne radar.

At just gone 9 pm the Defiant was directed towards a German over Sussex. Barwell spotted it when it was 500 ft above them and half a mile away. He closed to just 50 yards below and behind the Heinkel 111, at which point Martin opened fire. The German suddenly lurched upward, its nose pointing almost vertically, then it went into a steep dive. The Heinkel fell straight down into cloud and was lost to sight – though the flaming wreckage was found near Seaford.

Barwell and Martin landed to refuel, then went up again at 2 am. Two hours later they were once more directed to an intruder. This time the German crew saw the approaching Defiant, turned towards France and climbed towards some distant cloud. Barwell gave chase, but soon found himself the target of the German rear gunner and had to take evasive action. Undeterred, Martin managed to get off a few short bursts at extreme range. Sparks were seen coming from the German aircraft as Martin's bullets hit home. Then the German went into a vertical dive into the sea.

It had certainly been an exciting night, but the luck of Barwell and Martin had not changed for good. Despite flying long hours of night patrols they never again got close enough to a German bomber to open fire.

The crews of 264 were then given permission to try some experimental 'intruder' missions over northern France. These involved flying out soon after dusk to cruise around over the favoured routes of outbound Luftwaffe bombers in the hope of spotting and attacking one. The kill rate on such missions was low, but it was generally thought that the effort was worthwhile as it forced the Germans to be on edge from the moment they took off until the instant they landed. In the event the men of 264 did shoot down three Germans over France during May.

One of the successful crews was that of Flying Officer Fred Hughes and gunner Sergeant Fred Gash. At this date they were new and relatively inexperienced as combat air crew. Nevertheless, Hughes was awarded a

Taken by a photographer at an RAF base 'somewhere in southern England', this remarkable picture shows a Messerschmitt Bf110 in the act of dropping its bombs during a low-level high speed raid in 1941.

DFC and Gash a DFM for their work over the night skies of Kent in the spring of 1941. Two years later, by which time he was flying Beaufighters, Hughes would get a bar to his DFC for shooting down three enemy bombers over North Africa. In September 1943 Hughes went on to be awarded an astonishing second bar to his DFC, this time for destroying a further seven enemy aircraft in just two months.

In April 1941, a pilot who would become one of the most famous RAF men of them all came to serve with 29 Squadron, flying Beaufighters out of West Malling. This was Guy Gibson, who would win his Victoria Cross leading the famous Dambusters' raid in 1943. In 1941, however, he was taking a break from bombers to fly night-fighters.

One of Gibson's more action-packed nights came soon after he arrived in Kent. As usual the patrol started with long, tedious hours of circling, this time over Brighton, while the ground radar controllers tried to get a definite fix on a German aircraft. Long after midnight a German was located over Hove, and Gibson went in to the attack. He stalked the German, finally getting a visual fix when he saw the small flashes of flame coming out of the enemy's exhausts. A single burst caused the German bombs to explode in a flash that temporarily blinded Gibson.

A few minutes later the radar controller sent Gibson off after a second German. Again, Gibson stalked the intruder with his onboard air-to-air radar to get a visual fix. Just as Gibson was about to open fire, he saw the German aircraft flip on to its back and dive steeply away. Gibson and his radar operator, Sergeant James, watched it go down and crash into fields. Both men were puzzled by the way the German had gone down before they opened fire.

The German crew baled out and reported that they had been hit earlier in the night and had been heading for home when, unknown to them, Gibson began his stalk. They claimed that they had been hit by an object they took to be a cannon shell, which had smashed one wing to pieces. Neither Gibson nor any other pilot had fired at them, so the mystery remains.

One of the men described publicly as a 'wireless operator' (but really the radar operator) in Gibson's squadron was Sergeant Murray Ross, a cheerful Scot, whose jokes and wit did much to keep morale very high in this squadron. On one night mission just days after No.29 arrived in Kent, Ross's aircraft was attacking an intruder, when all four cannon suddenly jammed. Undeterred by the total dark and cramped conditions inside the Beaufighter's nose, Ross scrabbled about to remove the heavy ammunition pans and so get at the cannon.

After 25 minutes and a good deal of bad language, Ross announced that he had got three of the cannon working. Almost at once ground radar announced a new intruder in the area, which Ross soon picked up on his radar set and directed his pilot into a successful attack.

*Guy Gibson. Although better known for his exploits on bombers with
the Dambuster Squadron, Gibson spent several months flying
night-fighters out of Kent in the summer and autumn of 1941*

In April a period of good weather allowed Goering to mount a series of increasingly heavy and concentrated attacks on Plymouth, Southampton, Bristol and Birmingham, with London also receiving its share of raids. The press dubbed the onslaught the 'Little Blitz' while the British government began to wonder if it heralded a renewed Battle of Britain and perhaps even an invasion. The German campaign reached a climax on 10 May with a massive raid on London.

That night Guy Gibson was up in his Beaufighter, patrolling over south London. Four times he was vectored onto a German bomber, four times Sergeant James directed him into a firing position and four times the guns jammed. Gibson was furious and wrote a strongly worded note to the maintenance crews. Those mechanics then got to work, stripping down the guns and cannon but could find nothing wrong. Two nights later Gibson's guns jammed again, and again the ground crew were put to work, only to find nothing wrong.

It was not until 14 May that a mechanic thought to check the firing button itself, and found it to have a cracked wire that caused an intermittent fault. In the event it made little difference, Gibson was to stay on night-fighter duty until December of that year, but would not shoot down another German.

The reason was that quite suddenly on 17 May 1941 the Luftwaffe was gone. Where before there had been massed squadrons of bombers, fighters and fighter-bombers, there were now just a few units scattered across northern France. The large-scale formations of recent months were no more. Speculation was rife as to where the Luftwaffe had gone. Had Hitler called off his invasion of Britain? Was he about to offer a compromise peace? Was the Luftwaffe going to North Africa to support Mussolini's troops attacking British Egypt? Had Goering given them all a holiday? Nobody knew.

There were still German aircraft in France and the Low Countries, of course – about 500 of them. But the majority of these aircraft were fighters for the defence of German-occupied Europe, with only a few bombers for attacking Britain. The vast bulk of the Luftwaffe had been withdrawn.

Then, on 22 June 1941, the mystery of where the bulk of the Luftwaffe had gone was solved. Hitler launched the German armed forces on their invasion of Russia. The Luftwaffe was back to its favourite role of supporting a ground blitzkrieg as it had done in Poland in 1939 and France in 1940. Blasting the Soviet opposition to pieces, the bombers cleared the way for the dreaded panzer assault while the German fighters swept the skies clear of Russian aircraft. The first few months of the Russian war were a staggering success for the Luftwaffe and the German army. Vast swathes of territory were conquered, millions of enemy troops captured and the onward rush of the panzers barely slowed.

It was at about this time that some British pilots began to report the truly disturbing experience of being shot at by Spitfires. The experience of Sergeant Cox of 19 Squadron on 27 June is typical. He was part of an evening patrol of ten Spitfires over Gravelines that tangled with six Messerschmitt 109 fighters. As the combat ended, Cox saw two Spitfires some distance ahead and below him, so he dived down gently to take up formation with them for the flight back to Kent. He was astounded when the two aircraft suddenly turned and opened fire. Cox's engine was smashed and he was lucky to glide back over the Channel, coming down for a crashlanding in a damp meadow on Romney Marsh.

A Luftwaffe publicity photo issued in the summer of 1941 shows a Bf109 on the tail of a Spitfire over France. The original caption stressed the supposed superiority of the 109 in combat.

It later transpired that the problem was the introduction by the Luftwaffe of the F2 variant of the Messerschmitt Bf109. Unlike all earlier German fighters, which had square wingtips, this model had slightly pointed, round wingtips like those of the Spitfire. The RAF pilots had got so accustomed to identifying any square tipped wing as belonging to German fighters and any rounded or pointed wingtip as British that the new aircraft was causing immense confusion.

It was July before it was realised that the Germans had a new variant in action – and even then mistakes continued to be made. On 7 August Pilot Officer Scott, also of 19 Squadron, was returning home across the Channel after a patrol over the St Omer area when he saw what he took to be a Spitfire flying in a similar direction. He altered direction to come alongside the other aircraft. As he came level with the other aircraft, Scott noticed the 'Spitfire' had a brown cowling and nosecone. Unaware that such a paint scheme was being used by any squadron in Kent, Scott looked closer and suddenly realised that he was barely 50 ft from a Messerschmitt 109F. The German pilot seems to have realised at almost the same instant that he too had made a mistake of identification, as the 109 flinched sideways as if the pilot had suddenly jerked the control column. The German then dived into cloud and Scott lost him.

Back in the West, on the very day that Germany, Romania and Italy attacked Russia, 609 Squadron was sent up from Biggin Hill to fly a rodeo over northern France. This time they got the dogfight that this type of mission had been designed to provoke. Flying with 609 was Sergeant Tom Rigler, who had made a speciality of ground attack since joining the squadron from training school on 5 March. This time he did not have time for his habitually accurate strafing of airfields and military bases before the squadron was met by a force of 109s. In the wheeling dogfight that followed, Rigler sent no fewer than three German aircraft down, to the delight and surprise of his comrades.

By 28 August Rigler had destroyed three more German aircraft in the air, plus two more probables. He was awarded a DFM for his work and, when asked to comment on Rigler's actions, his squadron commander wrote 'He has shown outstanding keenness to seek out and destroy enemy aircraft in the air and an almost embarrassing enthusiasm to harass the enemy on the ground.'

Meanwhile, RAF Fighter Command was beginning to realise that things were not going all its own way. In June and July a total of 46 operations had been flown over France, during which 123 fighters had been lost. Unlike during the Battle of Britain when downed pilots were often able to return to their units, those men shot down over France were either killed or captured. In August even stronger escorts were being provided to circus operations, with an extra wing of three squadrons joining in by flying out after the others to meet them as they flew home and provide them with cover. Even so the high rate of losses continued.

Douglas decided that the main problem was that the operations had become too predictable and the Germans were prepared for them. He therefore reduced the number of operations being organised and insisted that they were spread out across all of northern France, rather than being concentrated on those areas that could be reached most quickly. That was to remain the pattern for the rest of the year.

The workload for Fighter Command pilots could be enormous. Between May and December 1941 Sergeant Robert Finn of 615 Squadron flew 48 missions over Britain or the Channel and another 43 over France. During that time he set one ship on fire, strafed five others, shot down a Heinkel floatplane that was laying mines in the Channel and destroyed an electricity power station. He was awarded a much-deserved DFM for what his wing commander termed 'a fine example of aggressive spirit'. Finn was not alone, many other pilots clocked up equally large numbers of sorties.

In July 1941, 29 Squadron was flying patrols over the Thames Estuary in their Beaufighters. Sergeant William Gregory was directed towards an intruder by ground radar control and soon picked up the German on his AI at 6,000 ft off the Isle of Sheppey. Guiding his pilot, Flight Lieutenant J. Braham, with some skill, Gregory brought the Beaufighter up on the German from below and behind. A quick burst was all that was required.

On 12 September, 29 Squadron's pairing of Gregory and Braham was back in action over the Thames. This time they were directed in by radar control with rather less skill than before and found themselves diving at great speed on a target that was stooging along very slowly. Despite the awkward approach, Gregory again got Braham into a good firing position and the pair were able to claim their second victim, whom they sent splashing down into the Thames.

One of the key characters from Kent at this time was Percy Lucas, known to all as 'Laddie'. Lucas was born in Sandwich, Kent, and grew into a champion sportsman. In 1935 he was the top amateur golf player

Westland Whirlwind

Type:	Twin engined, single seat fighter-bomber
Engine:	2 x Rolls Royce Peregine 1
Wingspan:	45 ft
Length:	32 ft 9 in
Height:	11 ft 9 in
Weight:	Empty 8310 lb
	Loaded 11,388 lb
Armament:	4 x 20 mm cannon in nose plus 2 x 500 lb bombs
Max speed:	360 mph
Ceiling:	30,000 ft
Range:	800 miles
Production:	112

Westland's Whirlwind was a superlative aircraft, but suffered from delays caused by its engine control system and so did not reach the RAF until early in 1941, instead of the planned late 1939. By that date its main armament of four 20 mm cannons had been matched by the latest versions of both the Spitfire and Hurricane, each of which had the edge over the Whirlwind at the high altitudes where German bombers flew. However, the Whirlwind was found to have magnificent performance at low altitudes, outperforming even the latest German fighters. Although production as a fighter was halted, the fighter-bomber variant was produced. In that role too, the Whirlwind would be surpassed by newer aircraft and by December 1941 its manufacture had been halted.

in Britain, a position he was to regain once the war was over, and began a career as a sports journalist. In 1936 he played in the Walker Cup and was so seasick when crossing to the USA that he swore never again to go to sea. So when war broke out, Laddie Lucas joined the RAF not the Royal Navy. He came out of pilot training in 1941 and was posted to 66 Squadron, flying Jim Crow patrols over the Channel.

Lucas was to earn his greatest fame after being sent to Malta in February

1942 to join 249 Squadron. In the following two months the German and Italian bombers dropped twice as many bombs on Malta as had hit London throughout the entire Blitz. The British fighters were always outnumbered, sometimes by up to 10:1, and Lucas was shot down several times.

He was awarded a DFC for breaking up an attack on Valetta in July 1942, by which time he had exchanged his old Hurricane for a new Spitfire. He led his squadron to attack three Italian bombers, only to find that no fewer than 80 Messerschmitt fighters were providing escort. Undeterred, Lucas led his Spitfires in a great curving loop that brought them into position above and in the sun from the Germans. He then led his formation in a steep dive straight through the German fighter formation and down onto the bombers, all of which were shot down. With the advantage of speed and surprise, the Spitfires got safely away before any German could react.

In 1943, Lucas returned to Britain to serve on the staff at Bentley Priory before getting back to operations with 616 Squadron. He later commanded the Spitfire Wing at Coltishall in Norfolk and then led 613 Squadron with its ground-attack Mosquitoes during the campaign across France and into Germany in 1944 and 1945.

After the war Lucas returned to Kent and to journalism, though in 1950 he entered Parliament and made a name for himself as an expert on aviation matters. Leaving politics in 1959 he took up writing full time. He died in 1998 with a DFC, DSO and bar and a CBE; surely one of the greatest heroes flying with Fighter Command that Kent was to produce.

Chapter 8

A Tiger by the Tail

In late 1941 some RAF pilots had reported seeing a new type of German fighter – the FW190 – that could fly faster, turn tighter and climb steeper than the then standard Messerschmitt Bf109. At first British intelligence officers could make little of the reports, based as they were on fleeting glimpses in combat situations. By the end of the year, however, it was clear that the Germans now possessed a fighter that was superior in every way to the Spitfires and Hurricanes of the RAF – and that it was entering service in increasing numbers. The RAF had a tiger by the tail.

The answer, or at least a partial answer, came in the form of the Spitfire MkIX. This had an uprated Merlin engine developing 1565 hp, as opposed to the 1030 hp of the engine in the Spitfire MkI. It was faster than the existing Spitfires, with an edge in terms of speed and height over the FW190. However, the Spitfire MkIX was less nimble than its opposition and could not climb as quickly. Each fighter had its advantages, but overall they were evenly matched.

A second new fighter joining the RAF in 1942 was the Hawker Typhoon. This was a larger, heavier aircraft but mounted a massively powerful engine. The RAF had high hopes for this machine, but it soon proved to be less effective at high altitude than had been hoped. Its performance at low altitude was, however, superlative.

The advent of the FW190 came at a bad time for Fighter Command. The

Big and heavy, the Hawker Typhoon could reach 412 mph with its enormously powerful Sabre engine. This was the first RAF aircraft able to reach 400 mph and it made an immediate impact when it entered service.

tempo of fighting in the Mediterranean was gathering pace, with a consequent increase in demand for fighters, and the sudden entry of Japan into the war in December 1941 meant that even more fighters had to be sent out to India, Burma and even Australia. As it was now clear that Hitler did not intend a major land invasion of Britain, Fighter Command found itself no longer the number one priority when it came to supplies of new aircraft.

With the numbers of fighters nothing like as great as Sholto Douglas wanted, he was nonetheless expected to continue protecting Britain from aerial attack and to launch raids on enemy territory. Bomber Command was by now stepping up its night offensive on the Reich, but Fighter Command had the task of mounting low fast raids on targets in northern France and the Low Countries.

Such raids could go unexpectedly awry, as a Beaufighter crew of 29 Squadron discovered on 27 January. Returning to West Malling, radio operator (and radar operator) Sergeant Henry Ellis received a message that his base could not be used, due to a very thick fall of snow. He was diverted to Hunsdon, only to find as he approached that snow was falling

A squadron sets out on a sweep over France in the summer of 1942, watched by a farm worker. By this date fighter sweeps were becoming increasingly dangerous operations.

heavily and visibility was down to 750 yards. Lacking fuel to go anywhere else, Ellis turned to the night landing equipment, advising his pilot to complete a circuit so that he could get his bearings properly. At this point an engine cut out. The pilot insisted on landing at once, so Ellis hunched over the complex equipment, shouting out instructions. The aircraft got down in one piece, landing straight on the runway. Ellis was awarded an immediate DFM for his work that night.

Then, in the spring of 1942, Douglas was confronted with a new task. Fighter Command had to begin preparing for an Allied invasion of France from Britain.

Fighter Command was not alone in this, as the army and navy were also ordered to begin planning for the so-called Second Front. On one thing everyone at the Allied high command was agreed: nobody really knew very much about either large scale amphibious assaults or German defences. The last time the British had landed troops from the sea onto a defended shoreline had been at Gallipoli in 1915, and that had turned into a disaster. There were plenty of ideas about what should be done and how, but nobody knew if they would work. What was needed was a test run. It was decided to launch a large-scale raid on the French coast. The target chosen was Dieppe.

Dieppe, seen from the air, with key features of the raid pointed out in white writing.

The idea of the Dieppe raid was to land 6,000 men, plus tanks and artillery both in the port and along beaches on either side. The town and harbour were to be captured intact and a defensive perimeter established – for when the real invasion took place a port would be needed. Having held the town for four hours, the force was to withdraw, demolishing anything of use to the Germans as they went.

Fighter Command's main task was to gain and hold total air superiority over Dieppe, the area immediately inland and the English Channel for the entire day. They also had the task of providing ground-attack aircraft to attack German defences, most importantly the heavy guns known to be positioned on the cliffs around the port. RAF Bomber Command would, meanwhile, bomb bridges and other targets inland, and keep some squadrons ready to attack any columns of German troops seen to be heading for Dieppe. The date was set for 19 August 1942, when the tides would be perfect.

Air Vice Marshal Sir Trafford Leigh-Mallory, who commanded 11 Group of Fighter Command in 1942. He was in charge of the air forces during the Dieppe raid.

Douglas and his commander of 11 Group, Leigh-Mallory, set to work planning their side of the raid. Several squadrons were moved from other groups to boost the strength available on the day. In all, Fighter Command had 48 Spitfire squadrons ready in Kent on the day, plus ten more of Hurricanes, Whirlwinds and Typhoons. While the overall operation would be run from 11 Group HQ, a forward combat control room was established on a ship that would be positioned just off Dieppe. The senior staff officer for 11 Group, Group Captain Harry Broadhurst, was to be sent up in a special high-altitude Spitfire to stooge about at 44,000 ft over Dieppe to keep an eye on things and stay in radio contact with 11 Group HQ.

A naval launch heads for Dieppe soon after dawn on the day of the raid. At this point the disastrous nature of the attack had not yet become clear.

The invasion fleet sailed before dawn, and Fighter Command likewise went into action as the cold grey light of dawn came up. Manston's 174 Squadron were the first into action. Equipped with Hurricanes fitted with underwing bombs, the pilots were to attack at tree-top height a battery of German heavy guns overlooking one of the landing beaches. The seventeen aircraft took off before dawn, timing the attack to take place as the sun lifted over the eastern horizon.

The Hurricane pilots had no trouble finding their target, but were met by a massive amount of light flak. Clearly the German defenders were both awake and ready to receive an attack. The squadron commander was shot down in flames, and two others went down. The remaining aircraft planted their bombs accurately, but the battery was only partly put out of action, as the entrenchments proved to be stronger than expected. Putting down as arranged at the advanced landing ground at Ford, the survivors of 174 found that every single aircraft had been damaged. The ground crew went to work and by 2 pm eight Hurricanes were fit to fly.

The second mission of the day for 174 Squadron was to attack a column of panzers heading for Dieppe from the Calais direction. The squadron crossed the Channel at 1,500 ft, then dropped down to 100 ft as they roared over the coast. The target was found with ease, but again flak was very heavy. One Hurricane blew up even before the attack was launched. A second, piloted by Free French officer du Fretay, was damaged and crashed straight into a panzer. A third, piloted by Sergeant J.W. Brooks, also hit a panzer, but escaped with a smashed undercarriage and the tank's radio aerial embedded in a wing. The survivors again headed for

Dieppe photographed from a naval ship offshore as the fighting reached a peak in mid-morning of the raid.

Ford, and had barely landed when a German Junkers Ju88 bomber came in low, bombing and strafing the airfield.

The Squadron had begun the day with seventeen pilots and aircraft fit for duty. By sunset there were only eight pilots uninjured and only four Hurricanes able to fly.

The Dieppe raid was the last time that the venerable Defiants saw action. By this date the turret-fighters had been taken off combat duties, even at night, and were being used for air-sea rescue tasks. Their role was to patrol at low height looking for any parachutes coming down, or to race to the last known location of a lost aircraft. If they managed to find aircrew in the sea, the Defiants were to radio the position to base so that a Walrus flying boat could come out to rescue the men. The Defiants were expected to drive off any German aircraft or boats that tried to intervene.

Between them, 277 and 515 Squadrons provided 21 Defiants for the Dieppe operation. One fighter pilot and one bomber crew were rescued by the Defiant/Walrus partnership. Thereafter the Defiants were seen no more over Kent, though they continued to patrol the North Sea from Lincolnshire, searching for downed bomber crews, until June 1943.

By 1942 the Air-Sea Rescue service had been perfected. Here a fighter pilot is about to be rescued from his dinghy by the crew of a flying boat.

In 1942, R.F. Hamlin became head of the RAF's Air-Sea Rescue service. By the end of the war many pilots of Fighter Command would owe their lives to his efficient organisation.

Fighter Command received a bad mauling in the skies over Dieppe. In all, 106 aircraft were lost or written off on return and 47 pilots killed. Despite putting up as many aircraft as possible Fighter Command had clearly failed to achieve control of the air over Dieppe or inland, though the skies over the Channel were secured. Douglas could console himself that his men claimed 96 German aircraft destroyed, though he would have known that the true figure was most likely smaller. That only 48 had actually been shot down was not discovered until after the war. On the

Two commandos photographed on their return from Dieppe. The flag was hoisted on the beach to guide in the landing-craft bringing the first assault wave.

ground things had gone even worse. Most tanks had failed to get ashore and the infantry had failed to capture most of their objectives. Half the men landed were killed or captured, nearly all of them Canadians.

Dieppe had been a bloody failure; however, important lessons had been learnt. When it came to the real invasion two years later the planners, including those of Fighter Command, would handle things very differently.

A new air threat emerged in the late summer as the Germans pushed forwards increasing numbers of Messerschmitt 109s and FW190s armed with bombs. These aircraft came over from France low and fast to bomb targets close to the south and east coasts of England, then raced back home. So fast did the raids happen that it proved very difficult for Fighter Command to react.

One RAF patrol was caught unawares by a formation of Messerschmitt 109s returning from a raid and spoiling for a fight. Pilot Officer Dougall spotted the German aircraft, but when he tried to alert his comrades to the fact he found his radio was not working. Dougall accelerated to cut in front of his startled commander, pointing desperately at the fast-approaching enemy fighters. He got his message across, but at the cost of laying himself wide open to attack and he was duly shot down. Fortunately he was not badly injured.

The monotonous grind of patrolling could be wearing. Flight Lieutenant Jack Humphreys of 29 Squadron, operating from West Malling, clocked up 232 hours of night flying in 127 operational flights in the year to October 1941. It was also dangerous. On 18 October, two Spitfires of 616 Squadron flew out of Hawkinge to patrol an area of the Channel. They were met by a formation of four FW190s and a dogfight ensued. One German and one British aircraft were shot down.

As the remaining Germans peeled away, Pilot Officer Ronald Large saw his comrade drifting down into the sea by parachute. As Large circled, the downed pilot inflated his yellow dinghy and scrambled aboard. Large radioed the location to base so that a patrol boat could pick up his comrade and then, short on fuel, raced for the nearest air base. He landed and demanded to be refuelled instantly and dashed back into the air without waiting for his aircraft to be rearmed.

Racing back over the Channel, Large found his friend's dinghy and began circling so that the patrol boat could find the tiny craft. Unfortunately for Large, his conspicuously circling Spitfire was spotted not only by the British boat, but also by a flight of German fighters. They

The pilots of 403 Squadron, Royal Canadian Air Force, which flew out of Manston during the autumn of 1942. (Manston S&H Mem)

Flying Officer Roy Wozniak (in the cockpit) with other pilots of 403 Squadron, Royal Canadian Air Force, which flew from Manston in 1942. (Manston S&H Mem)

came roaring down with guns firing. Without any ammunition, Large had no choice but to weave, dive and turn at high speed as he raced for home. He made it.

Another pilot to help aircrew ditched in the drink was Sergeant Ronald Stillwell of 65 Squadron. In August 1941 he had spotted an RAF bomber in the sea off the Dutch coast and circled while the crew got into a dinghy. He then radioed the location to base, enabling the crew to be rescued. In April 1942 he spotted a pilot in the sea, supported only by his life jacket. Stillwell again circled the site to radio the position. This time he managed to manoeuvre his own dinghy out of its stowed position, throw back the cockpit canopy and heave the dinghy overboard so that it splashed down just fifteen yards from the floating pilot. Tragically, the downed pilot later died of his wounds.

On 31 October 1942 a whole new chapter opened in the story of German raids on Britain. The day began quietly enough; Fighter Command had three Spitfires from Biggin Hill flying in the Channel circling over a convoy of ships moving east, but otherwise no aircraft were up. It was not until 4.50 pm that radar picked up any German aircraft – a lone bomber over Calais heading towards Hythe. At 5.05 pm this single aircraft had reached Hythe and the local Observer Corps were alerted. They reported back that there were twenty German aircraft, not one. At almost the same moment one of the Spitfire pilots escorting the convoy sent back a frantic radio message. 'My God,' he yelled back to Biggin Hill, 'there are hundreds of the bastards coming. For Christ's sake get somebody up here.'

The fighter squadrons of Kent were sent orders to scramble into the air, while frantic messages were sent to radar plotters to ask what was going on. The radar operators scanned the skies, but could pick up no trace of the crowds of enemy aircraft seen by both the Spitfire pilot and Observer Corps.

Meanwhile, the startled Spitfire pilot over the convoy was relieved to see the massed formations of Germans ignoring both him and his convoy. They were after other targets. A total of 48 British fighters were by now in the air. The bulk of the Germans were heading for Canterbury, but smaller formations were making raids on Hawkinge, Manston and Dover. The fighters made for the force going for Canterbury and, although no Germans were shot down, their formation was disrupted and their aim spoiled. One Spitfire was destroyed, though the pilot escaped unscathed.

A sneak raid on Canterbury in the spring of 1942 demolished the ancient medieval library of the cathedral.

Focke Wulf FW190

Type:	Fighter
Engine:	1 x 1700 hp BMW 801D
Wingspan:	34 ft 5 in
Length:	29 ft
Height:	13 ft
Weight:	Empty 6393 lb
	Loaded 8770 lb
Armament:	2 x 7.9 machine guns in nose plus 4 x 20 mm
	cannon in wings
Max speed:	382 mph
Ceiling:	35,000 ft
Range:	500 miles
Production:	20,051

Without doubt Germany's finest fighter of the war, the Focke Wulf FW190 first flew in June 1939 but problems with the engine meant it did not enter combat in great numbers until the end of 1941. It proved to be fast and nimble, easily outclassing all Allied fighters – even the Spitfire MkV, which had only just entered service. The British rushed the Spitfire IX into production, but this took time and only matched the FW190 in combat conditions. By the end of 1942, half of all German fighters being produced were FW190s, designed in a number of variants to carry bombs or torpedoes as well as the standard fighter armament. In 1944 a variant, the FW190D was produced with a Junkers Jumo 213 engine. This aircraft proved to be a magnificent high-altitude fighter and took a heavy toll of American daylight bombers operating above 30,000 ft. The FW190G was a ground attack variant able to carry up to 4,000 lb of bombs to a range of 220 miles from base.

It had been a bad day for Fighter Command. An inquiry was set up to try to find out what had gone wrong and how to put it right. It was realised that the absence of a radar echo was due to a jamming device having been switched on in France. Somehow the Germans had learnt how

Hawker Typhoon

Type: Fighter-bomber
Engine: 1 x 2180 hp Napier Sabre II
Wingspan: 41 ft 7 in
Length: 31 ft 11 in
Height: 15 ft 3 in
Weight: Empty   8840 lb
                 Loaded   13,980 lb
Armament: 12 x .303 in machine guns or 4 x 20 mm cannon in wings,
                 plus 2 x 500 lb bombs or 8 x 3 in rockets under wings.
Max speed: 412 mph
Ceiling: 31,800 ft
Range: 980 miles
Production: 3330

The Typhoon was almost not built at all. The early prototypes all suffered from bent and warped airframes just in front of the tail when put through dogfight manoeuvres, and it was not until extensive changes had been introduced that the aircraft was safe to fly. When it entered service in the summer of 1942 pilots soon found that the Typhoon was hopelessly outclassed at high altitudes by German fighters, though it had the edge at under around 5,000 ft. By 1943 the Typhoon – by now widely nicknamed the Tiffy – had become a dedicated ground attack aircraft. Its formidable hitting power and low-altitude performance made it superlative in this role. No fewer than 26 squadrons were equipped with Typhoons in time for D-Day in June 1944. It remained in production until November 1945.

to render radar inoperative, but only over a relatively small area. It was decided to disperse some fighters to forward landing grounds at dawn each day to enable them to get into the air quickly if needed.

Fighter Command continued with its regular tasks and on 2 November rodeo No.107 was flown. From Biggin Hill, 611 Squadron took off, flying low over the Channel to the mouth of the Somme and then climbing for height over Abbeville before heading north to join 340 Squadron, which

was coming south. Over Berck the two squadrons met a force of FW190s and a dogfight ensued. Wing Commander Thomas, commanding 611 Squadron, shot down two FW190s, while Flying Officer de Tedesco downed a third. Two Spitfires also went down and a third pilot was badly wounded, but got his aircraft home.

It had been an eventful, and not untypical rodeo mission. Not all flights ended with success, however. Rodeo No. 109 saw 611 Squadron flying over Calais at 23,000 ft. They met fifteen FW190s and engaged in a dogfight. Despite the expenditure of thousands of rounds of ammunition by both sides, nobody was killed. One FW190 was seen to be damaged, but the pilot bailed out and landed safely.

Circus No.242 on 12 December proved to be memorable for the wrong reasons. No.611 Squadron was flying out to meet four squadrons of American B17 'Flying Fortress' bombers returning from a raid on Rouen. The British fighters got to the rendezvous before the Americans, so they pushed on to meet the bombers near Beauvais. The Americans, not expecting to meet their escort until some while later, mistook the approaching fighters for Germans and opened fire. Fortunately nobody was hurt, but the radio airwaves were thick with the most appalling language.

Bad weather then closed in and halted the missions planned by Fighter Command for the rest of the year.

Chapter 9

Escort Duty

The campaign of 1943 opened with major changes on both sides of the Channel. In England, RAF Fighter Command gained a new commander in the shape of Air Marshal Sir Trafford Leigh-Mallory, who was transferred from No.11 Group to take over. Leigh-Mallory reached the top of Fighter Command just as some serious and major decisions had to be taken.

The first of these was to decide on the future equipment of the command. The emphasis for Fighter Command was changing from defending Britain to preparing for the planned invasion of mainland Europe. This involved both launching fast, hit-and-run ground attacks close to the coast and providing escorts for bomber aircraft making longer range, heavier attacks.

The task of defending Britain was increasingly being handled by the Beaufighter at night and Spitfire during the day, with help from the Mosquito after dark and the Typhoon at low level. Increasingly the Typhoon was being seen as the way forward for ground attack. Although the disaster at Dieppe and supply problems meant that no invasion of France would take place in 1943, the planners were already looking forward to the day when they would need ground-attack aircraft to operate in close co-operation with armies on the ground. Hawker had already begun work on the Tempest, an improved Typhoon.

The Hawker Tempest was the last of the Hawker fighters to enter combat in the war. At low altitude this was the fastest Allied fighter in service, a fact its pilots used to good effect.

That left only the problem of bomber escorts. The Spitfire MkV was useful for close escort duty, breaking up attacking German fighter formations, but was outclassed in fighter vs fighter combats by the new German models. Only the Spitfire MkIX could handle the German fighters on their own terms, and the restricted range of the MkIX meant it could operate only close to bases in England.

Leigh-Mallory wanted some of the new P51 Mustangs as long-range fighters, but the Americans insisted that their own 8th Air Force should take priority for supply. Given that the 8th Air Force was flying long-range bombing missions over the Reich in daylight hours, while the RAF Bomber Command flew at night, they had a point, though Leigh-Mallory disagreed with them.

Meanwhile there had also been changes on the German side. The increasing weight of British attacks on German cities had led Hitler to demand reprisal attacks on British cities. Goering was, by this point, no longer the major figure in Reich politics that he had been. The failure of the Luftwaffe to win the Battle of Britain had annoyed Hitler, while the Luftwaffe's even more disastrous failure to supply German armies in Stalingrad by air had led to his disgrace and virtual retirement. The Luftwaffe was therefore in no position either to refuse Hitler's demands or to get the equipment they needed to carry them out.

By January 1943, when the new offensive was to begin, the Germans facing Britain had been given only 120 new bombers. These were the latest designs of Dornier and Junkers, but the vast bulk of the aircraft about to attack Britain were old models. Hitler was sending his best equipment to face Russia.

On 17 January the Luftwaffe sent 118 bombers to attack London. Six bombers were shot down that night. The new campaign became dubbed the 'mini blitz' by the British press. It continued through February and March but by April the Luftwaffe staff were looking for reasons not to send out raids, bad weather being a favourite. Fighter Command was simply taking too heavy a toll for the campaign to be sustained. By the end of May the short length of the nights was a good enough excuse for the attacks to be called off entirely.

On 20 January the assembled staff of Biggin Hill were settling down to lunch when the air raid siren sounded and the tannoy loudly announced that enemy bombers were coming in to attack. The pilots of 611 Squadron raced for their Spitfires, while most other people headed for the shelters. The 37 bomb-carrying FW190s and Messerschmitt Bf109s were on Biggin Hill before a single Spitfire could get aloft. Several bombs rained down over the northern half of the airfield as the Germans strafed the ground with their machine guns. The German aircraft tore off north-west, dropping more bombs on to Bromley before veering south. One of those bombs hit a school, killing a teacher and 45 children.

Meanwhile 611 were in the air and thirsting for revenge. The commander, Wing Commander Milne, led the aircraft to a position high over Beachy Head believing that the Germans would pass that way; he was right. It was just before 1 pm when Milne led his Spitfires into a screaming dive at the intruders. Milne selected a 109 for his attack, 'I fired two bursts from very close range, the first hitting the wing tip and the second the cockpit. The enemy aircraft blew up and went into the sea. I went after two remaining 109s and fired from about 300 yards and hit the port enemy aircraft in the radiator. I saw the trail of glycol left by it and it hit the sea.'

The Spitfire MkXII had clipped wingtips to improve performance at low altitudes and a Griffon IV engine. It was introduced in February 1943, specifically to counter low-level hit-and-run raids by bomber variants of the Fw190. Only 100 of this model were built to fill this role.

In all the Spitfires accounted for one FW190 and five Messerschmitt 109s without losing a single aircraft themselves.

Among the new models of German bomber coming over was the Dornier Do217, a development of the old Do17. Although of the same basic configuration as the older bomber, the Do217 had a deeper fuselage, was able to carry more bombs, and was a larger, heavier aircraft overall. The fighter pilots of Kent soon noticed the new bomber and, on 15 February, the Beaufighter piloted by Flight Lieutenant John Atkinson of 609 Squadron sighted one south of London on its return to France.

The night was one of unremitting bad weather, and Atkinson had been on the point of calling off his patrol when the German came up on the radar screen. Atkinson steered so as to creep up on the German, but the enemy was alert and spotted him. The stormclouds were towering and flashing with lightning – threatening to ice up the wings of the two aircraft as they chased each other in deadly fashion through the skies. Atkinson got off a number of bursts of fire during the chase, but no hits were seen. Eventually the German dived into cloud and Atkinson was unable to find him again. Atkinson was luckier in March, when he shot down an unidentified German twin-engined bomber over the Channel. It was his 45th night mission in six months.

Then, on 2 April 1943, the Beaufighter from 85 Squadron with Sergeant Arthur Grimstone as radar operator was vectored onto a Do217 as it crossed the coast. The Beaufighter was able to approach the German without being seen and opened fire at point-blank range. The new bomber turned over slowly, then dived vertically to crash down into the ground. The boffins, as the RAF crews called scientists of all persuasions, rushed to the site but the Do217 had been so thoroughly destroyed that they were unable to learn anything from the wreckage.

The boffins had rather better luck on 19 May. The pilots of 609 Squadron were sitting around in the spring sunshine outside the dispersal hut at RAF Manston waiting to be sent up if any German aircraft arrived. One of them noticed a single-engined fighter coming in to land and idly watched as it dropped its wheels and swept down on to the runway. Then he noticed something odd about the new arrival. 'Bloody Hell,' the pilot shouted. 'It's a 190!' The other pilots looked up and, sure enough, the fighter now taxiing calmly across the airfield was one of the dreaded FW190 fighters.

Instantly all was movement and excitement. Some men rushed to their aircraft, others grabbed pistols, still others leapt into vehicles to block the

runway. Astonishingly the German pilot pulled up in front of the hut, switched off his engine and threw back the cockpit cover. Only then did he seem to realise that he was on an RAF base, by which time it was too late.

The pilot, Heinz Erhardt, had been flying a low-level hit-and-run raid on East Anglia. He had completed his mission without trouble, but his compass had then malfunctioned. Steering by the sun he had headed south, but was further to the west than he thought himself. He left the coast somewhere near Clacton and flew over a wide stretch of open sea. When he crossed another coast over a small town he thought he was over Calais or perhaps Dunkirk, but in fact was over Margate. Deciding to put down at the first airfield he saw to ask for directions home, Erhardt came in to land at Manston.

His capture was a boon, not so much for his own value but because he had delivered to the RAF a pristine and undamaged FW190. The boffins eagerly tore the aircraft apart to discover the secrets of its design and manufacture.

The unfortunate Luftwaffe pilot Heinz Erhardt (left) who landed his Fw190 fighter at Manston, thinking that he was at Calais. (RAF Manston Mus)

Meanwhile Biggin Hill was agog with excitement. The station's scoreboard now stood at 998 enemy aircraft claimed as destroyed by fighters flying out of Biggin Hill since the war began. Both 611 and 340 Squadrons were in residence, flying Spitfires, and the pressure was on to get the score up to 1,000 as quickly as possible. No other base in the world was even close to such a score. For several days the Biggin Hill Spitfires were ordered to fly escort missions for American Flying Fortress bombers. Such missions were essential, but notoriously dull, as the German fighters usually did not attack the bombers when escorts were around.

A B17 Flying Fortress of the USA 8th Air Force flies away from a target in France that it has just plastered with bombs. The year 1943 was increasingly taken up for the pilots of Fighter Command with flying escort missions for daylight bombers such as this.

Then, on 15 May, the two squadrons were ordered to join circus No.297. This mission saw six Mitchell bombers and eight Typhoons attacking Caen airfield, escorted by the two squadrons of Spitfires. On this occasion, the Germans came up to contest the issue. A force of FW190s approached from the south and dived to attack the Mitchells.

Among the British fighter pilots going into the attack was Squadron Leader J. Charles of 611 Squadron. He opened fire on one German and saw bits fly off its wing as his bullets took effect; then he was past the German and closed in on a second. He opened fire at 180 yards, setting the enemy on fire. This time Charles followed the enemy down to make sure, but he need not have bothered. The German pilot must have been killed for the FW190 dived straight into the ground. That brought the Biggin Hill score up to 999. It was only after the fighters returned to Biggin Hill that it was revealed that the first aircraft at which Charles had fired had also been shot down, as was confirmed by Flight Lieutenant Checketts, who saw it go down. Biggin Hill had its 1,000th kill.

The commander of this fateful circus was Wing Commander Al Deere, one of the most colourful fighter heroes to fly out of Kent. Born in New Zealand, Deere joined the RAF in 1937, and in 1939 his squadron, No.54, became one of the first to be equipped with Spitfires. Soon after war was declared the oxygen supply on his Spitfire failed during a high-altitude patrol, causing Deere to black out. He came to some minutes later as the sea filled the view in front of him. Hauling desperately on the joystick, Deere narrowly avoided a watery grave.

Deere entered action on 23 May 1940 when escorting a transport aircraft heading for Calais. He was attacked by a pair of Messerschmitt 109s, and succeeded in shooting them both down. That afternoon he shot down a third German fighter, accounting for his fourth the next morning and two more the day after that. That evening he himself was shot down, crash-landing on a Belgian beach and being pulled from the burning wreckage by a British soldier on his way to Dunkirk. Deere got back to Britain from the beaches of Dunkirk and returned to duty in time for the opening of the Battle of Britain. As he walked into his squadron's officers' mess a fellow pilot looked up and called out, 'Are you all right, Deere?' Deere grinned, 'Yes, darling,' he replied.

On 9 July he collided with a 109 during a dogfight and crash-landed again, this time in a field in Kent. Six days later he was shot down, bailing out at low level. Three days later he was shot down a third time – this time by a Spitfire, the pilot of which shot first and identified later. In August he was attacked by a 109 when taking off. His Spitfire flipped over, and Deere was left dangling helplessly from his seat straps until ground crew got him clear.

In September, Deere and his squadron were sent to Ayr in Scotland to rest and train up replacement pilots. The following year one of these pilots accidentally collided with Deere's aircraft on a training flight. Deere bailed out and parachuted down into the cesspit of a cattle farm. A few days later he was sent up to attack a lone German aircraft picked up by radar as it came in off the North Sea. Deere failed to catch up with the German aircraft before the pilot inexplicably baled out and the aircraft crashed. It later transpired that the mystery German had been Hitler's deputy Rudolf Hess on his strange solo peace mission.

After touring the USA in 1942 giving talks and lectures to civilians and USAAF personnel, Deere took over at Biggin Hill. He later joined the staff of 11 Group and returned to command Biggin Hill when peace came – by which time he had shot down a confirmed 22 enemy aircraft, got 10 probables and damaged another 18. He remained in the RAF after the war, becoming ADC to the Queen in 1961 and retiring in 1967 to become the civilian head of the RAF sports team. He died in 1995. It was a startling career for a Kiwi shepherd boy.

During the summer of 1943 Fighter Command stepped up its low-level raids into northern France. Although the Typhoon was becoming the favoured aircraft for such work, the Spitfire was also used. Indeed, 611 Squadron began

The exploits of the ground crew are generally overshadowed by those of the aircrew, but their work was tiring and demanding, and very often interrupted by enemy attacks. Harry Whiteley served at Manston from1943 to 1945. He had been a cinema projectionist in civilian life. (Manston S&H Mem)

Evelyn Dunn and another of the nurses who served at RAF Manston. The nurses cared for the sick as well as the wounded, working long hours to bring relief to those in their care. (Manston S&H Mem)

to earn itself a bit of a reputation as a train-buster squadron. The commander himself, Squadron Leader Walter Gibb, accounted for seven locomotives in July. By contrast, 609 Squadron favoured ships. In August the squadron sank or badly damaged no fewer than fifteen ships in the North Sea.

Not that the Typhoons were being eclipsed. No.1 Squadron was re-equipped with the powerful fighter and, after a few weeks of training, moved to Lympne in March. They were soon in action, attacking a German destroyer moving up the Channel on 9 April. The Typhoons specialised in attacking targets near the coast while the Spitfires of 609 Squadron – also based at Lympne – hovered above to tackle any German fighters. By November, Flying Officer Harrison Mossip had become No.1's champion train-buster, having accounted for nineteen locomotives as well as ten ships or boats.

In October, Hitler noticed that the nights were getting longer again. He ordered the Luftwaffe once more to begin nocturnal attacks on British cities. Again the German bombers took steady casualties for minimal results.

The aircrew of a Mosquito night-fighter squadron are given their final briefing before taking off for the night's mission protecting Britain from nocturnal Luftwaffe bombers.

A Mosquito NFII sits on the tarmac at sunset. This was the most numerous night-fighter version of the Mosquito in 1943, 270 having been built.

Under a full moon the air crew of a night-fighter squadron
wait beside a Mosquito to get the orders to take off to
meet an incoming German raid.

The new wave of attackers was, on the night of 21 October, welcomed by an 85 Squadron Mosquito night-fighter flown by Flight Leiutenant B. Thwaite, with Flying Officer William Clemo as radar operator. When they took off that evening the duo had already flown almost 40 missions and shot down two confirmed and one probable victim. Soon afterwards they were directed towards a contact over the North Sea. Clemo got a fix and directed Thwaite in on a textbook approach. A quick burst of fire sent the

Junkers Ju88

Type: Four-crew bomber
Engines: 2 x 1200 hp Junkers Jumo 211B
Wingspan: 59 ft 11 in
Length: 47 ft 2 in
Height: 15 ft 10 in
Weight: Empty 21,717 lb
Loaded 30,865 lb
Armament: 6 x 7.92 mm machine guns in nose, dorsal and
ventral positions plus 4,400 lb of bombs
Max speed: 292 mph
Ceiling: 26,900 ft
Range: 1696 miles
Production: 7000

The Junkers Ju88 was designed as a high-speed medium bomber in 1936 and it was this variant of the Ju88 that featured most in the Battle of Britain. This Ju88A was designed to be able to carry a fairly heavy bomb load on conventional level bombing missions, but also to be able to deliver a lighter bomb load when dive-bombing. It entered service with the Luftwaffe in August 1939, but was not used much in the Polish campaign as the crews were still getting used to its handling characteristics. It entered combat on 26 September with an attack on British shipping off the Scottish coast, and thereafter was seen in increasingly large numbers over the Western Front. The Ju88 was later produced in a bewilderingly large number of variants and models, totalling 15,000 aircraft in all. There were torpedo bombers, night-fighters, reconnaissance aircraft, maritime patrol bombers and ground attack versions. Production continued right up until the day before the Americans captured the Junkers factory in March 1945.

enemy into a vertical dive towards the sea. Minutes later a second blip flared up on the radar screen and again Clemo directed Thwaite into the attack. A second German went down less than ten minutes later, a quite remarkable feat.

Chapter 10

The Great Invasion

As 1944 opened, the long-planned invasion of France by combined British, American and Empire armies was becoming close to reality. England was groaning under the weight of men, tanks, guns and supplies – a contemporary joke had it that southern England might soon sink.

By January 1944 Fighter Command had achieved a clear superiority over the Luftwaffe in the skies over Britain, the North Sea, the Low Countries and northern France. That superiority had not yet become the total control of the skies that the planners of D-Day demanded but things were moving in the right direction. Yet even as the Luftwaffe was being defeated in the skies, Fighter Command was broken up.

On 15 November 1943 RAF Fighter Command was divided into two. The night-fighter Beaufighters and Mosquitoes, plus the older models of Spitfire and other fighters, were formed into the Air Defence of Great Britain (ADGB) force. Their task was to defend the skies over Britain from attack by German bombers by day or night.

The increasingly effective ground attack Typhoons and Hurribombers were allocated to the 2nd Tactical Air Force (TAF), along with some lighter bombers from Bomber Command. Their role was to attack those targets on the Continent that it was necessary to destroy before the invasion could take place. These were chiefly transport links, but also coastal defences and supply depots.

The commander of Fighter Command, Leigh-Mallory, was transferred to take over the 2nd TAF. The ADGB was given to Air Marshal Sir Roderic Hill; he would soon be very busy.

Soon after dusk on 17 January 1944 British radar stations began to pick up large formations of German aircraft taking off from the Low Countries and Denmark. Then everything suddenly went blank. The Germans had developed a new and highly effective method of jamming radar, which they named *Düppel*. Behind that mask a total of 227 bombers flew towards London.

Fortunately for the British, the jamming affected only the ground-based radar, not the air-to-air radar sets carried by the Beaufighter and Mosquito night-fighters. In total 25 German aircraft were brought down by anti-aircraft guns or night-fighters. This loss rate of over ten per cent could not be sustained, but the new assault had been ordered personally by Hitler.

This Steinbock offensive was designed to damage cities and towns in England in the hope that this would somehow delay the expected Allied invasion of France. In fact it caused the deaths of 1,556 civilians, and seriously injured more than 3,000. The losses to the Luftwaffe were heavy, around 300 bombers shot down out of 700 employed. The offensive petered out in early May.

Meanwhile, the men of what had been Fighter Command were called upon to undertake new and very dangerous missions, code-named 'Noballs'. There was no official explanation for these missions, but they involved low-level attacks on a particular type of target located in northern France. These consisted of two single-storey huts beside which stood a concrete ramp about 50 yards long. They were usually tucked away in woodland or hidden among farm buildings and were always heavily defended. The aircrew called upon to attack and destroy these targets speculated about what they might be, but no one really knew.

It was on one such mission that Ken Woodhouse of 401 Squadron was lost over France. He had been flying escort in his Spitfire MkIX when the engine suddenly stopped and he was forced to bail out. He landed in a field to be met by a 14-year-old farmboy, Marc Rendu. The boy helped Woodhouse to bury his parachute, then led him to the house of his grandfather, Wilfred Rendu. The older Rendu was in touch with the local French Resistance and two days later Woodhouse was bundled into the back of a farmtruck to be taken to Beauvais. There he met the Resistance

proper and by various routes was taken to the home of Olympe Vasseur in Paris, where he met an American pilot named Keith Suter.

Woodhouse and Suter were moved around Paris several times, never staying more than two nights in any one place. Eventually they were introduced to Maurice Cavalier, a master forger who had joined the Resistance and was now putting his clandestine skills to patriotic use. He gave Woodhouse and Suter forged identity cards belonging to men from Brittany, plus a train ticket to St Brieuc in Brittany. Woodhouse and Suter were then sent on their way accompanied by a young woman who went with them to St Brieuc, but did not get off the train there.

Woodhouse and Suter were wondering what they should do on the strange railway platform, when an elderly farmer winked at them and beckoned. They followed him to a house where they were fed and hidden until dusk. Another nameless guide then appeared and led the two airmen over fields and along lanes for two days, until they reached a remote barn. Inside were no fewer than 35 other Allied airmen. It transpired that the barn was near the coast. That night the airmen were led down a steep cliff path in darkness to a small beach where two rowing boats were waiting to take them out to a Royal Navy patrol boat a mile or so off shore. Before dawn the men were all safely in Dartmouth.

On 4 June the gates at airfields all across Britain were locked shut, all leave and permission to leave base was cancelled and armed guards set to enforce the isolation. The next day aircrew were told that the invasion was on for that night, and were given their orders. These involved a complex series of patrols that had to be carried out with great precision regarding both time and location. The Luftwaffe in the west may have been but a shadow of its former self, but it was by no means defeated. The patrols were designed to ensure that every section of the invasion area was protected by fighters at all times. Quite apart from any fighting that might be involved, the pilots were going to be driven to the edge of exhaustion by the need to stay in the air for hours, land, refuel and go back to the endless patrols.

In the event, D-Day proved to be remarkably quiet for the fighter pilots of the RAF. The Luftwaffe made no serious attempt to intervene in the invasion unfolding on the beaches of Normandy. Indeed, the Luftwaffe was soon pummelled into ineffectiveness by the destruction of their bases and the strangulation of supply lines, which meant the aircraft often had no fuel.

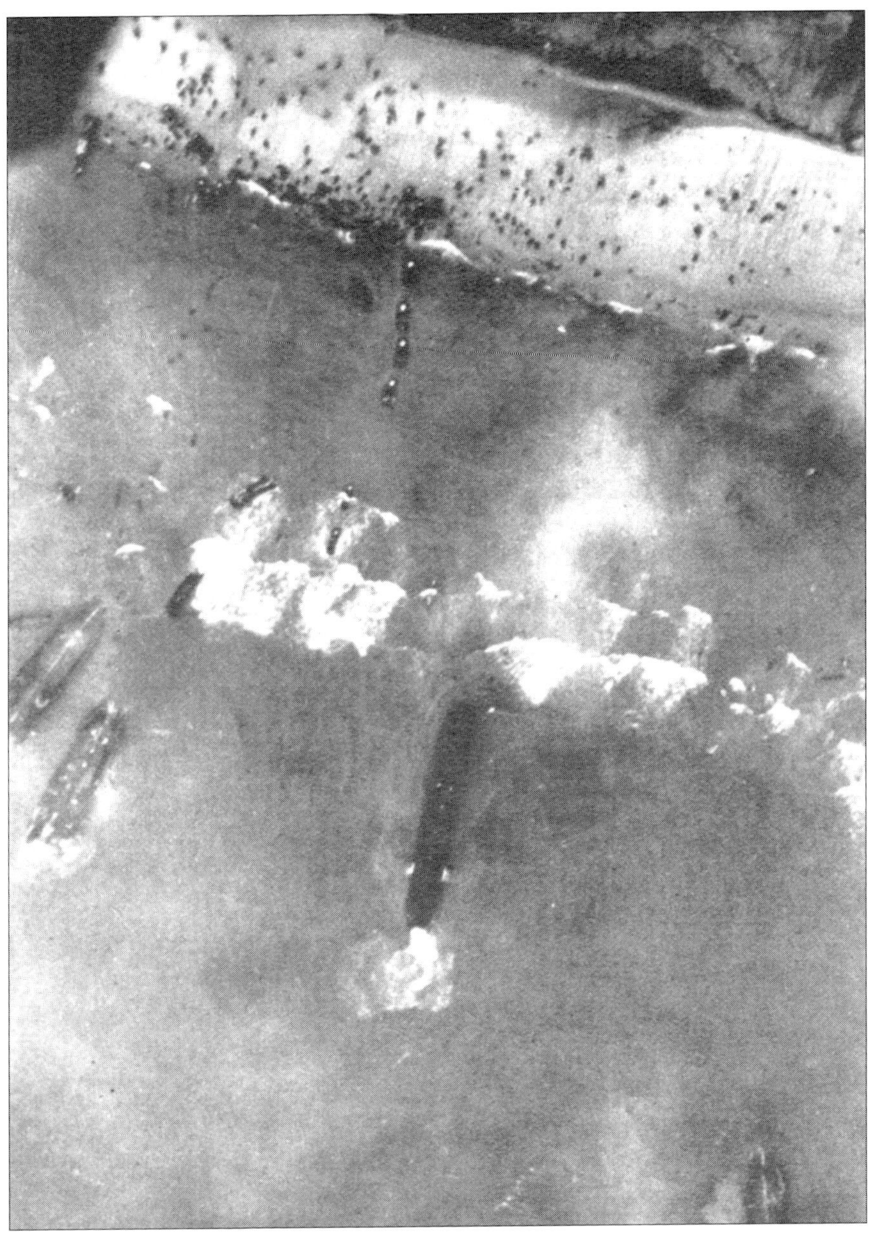

Gold Beach around mid-afternoon on D-Day, as photographed by an RAF reconnaissance aircraft. The landing craft can be seen offshore, while surf breaks over German obstacles. The dark dots on the beach are men and equipment.

On the third day after D-Day a beachmaster issues his instructions to get men and equipment being unloaded from the ships off Sword Beach. A light anti-aircraft gun can be seen behind him and a barrage balloon floats overhead. The constant patrols flown by RAF fighters made such precautions almost redundant.

Although despite such handicaps, the Luftwaffe did attack. They flew single missions at low level, hoping to get in, strike and get out again before the Allied fighters could intervene. On 22 June, Squadron Leader William Douglas of 611 Squadron was over the Normandy beachhead when he spotted a Junkers Ju88 on just such a mission. He dived to attack, but found that his gunsight fell off as soon as he tried to use it. Undeterred, Douglas closed to extremely close range, despite the fire from the German, aimed his nose at the bomber and opened fire. The bullets smashed into the German, which then exploded. Douglas and his aircraft were showered with burning debris. Despite some serious damage to his fighter, Douglas got back to England.

American combat troops rush ashore on Omaha Beach late on D-Day. This beach saw the fiercest fighting of the day.

A V1 races through the sky. The distinctive sound made by the engine was likened to a motorbike without a silencer. When the sound was heard people would scan the skies for a sight of the flying bomb.

On 13 June an outpost of the Observer Corps on the Kent coast reported a strange new German aircraft. For a start it produced a very strange sound, rather like a motorbike without a silencer labouring to get up a steep hill. And it was very small, though it is notoriously difficult to gauge the size of a flying object accurately. Finally there seemed to be neither cockpit nor propeller. The puzzled observer telephoned his report back to base. A few minutes later there was a terrific explosion at Gravesend, though no enemy bombers were in the sky overhead.

It may have been a puzzle to those on the ground, but to the intelligence officers it came as no surprise. The strange aircraft had been launched from one of the equally mysterious 'Noball' sites in northern France. It was a V1, the buzzbomb or doodlebug, which would become so familiar over southern England in the following months.

The V1 was officially the Vergeltungswaffe 1, 'revenge weapon No.1', that had been ordered by Hitler to be developed with the sole purpose of terrorising the British population into surrender. It was a simple pilotless aircraft powered by a ramjet that could get it up to 400 mph in level flight. The V1 had a simple gyroscope to keep it on a predetermined course and

A V1 is trundled towards its launch ramp by German soldiers. The sudden onslaught on Britain by this pilotless flying bomb came just days after D-Day.

flew straight and level until its fuel gave out, at which point it fell to earth. The nose carried a 2,000 lb warhead, much larger than any German bomb dropped during the Blitz.

That first day four of the V1 bombs crossed the English coast, aimed at London. Hill, in command of ADGB, had been informed some time earlier that some kind of flying bomb was about to be unleashed, but it was not until the V1s began arriving that anyone had a firm idea of how they would behave. Hill had set up a defensive system based on anti-aircraft guns, balloons trailing cables and his fighters. He hoped that it would be enough.

Children being evacuated from London in July 1944. The V weapon offensive caused civilian casualties to rise alarmingly, just as people had begun to think that air raids were a thing of the past.

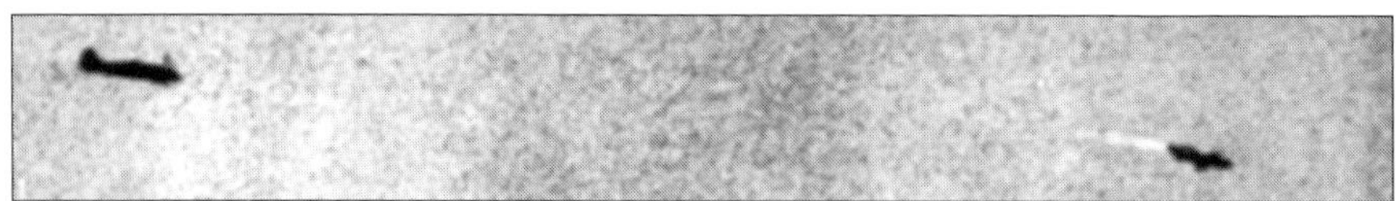

An RAF fighter chases a V1 across the skies of southern England. Such sights became relatively common in the summer of 1944.

On 15 June a total of 244 V1s were fired at Britain, and Hill quickly realised that his defences had a problem. The incoming weapons flew so low and fast that only the Typhoon, Tempest and Spitfire MkXIV could catch them. Meanwhile the anti-aircraft gunners had only a fleeting chance to bring down a V1, so early identification was crucial.

Hill's response was to put his guns along the coast, pointing towards France, and give them orders to shoot at anything flying low and fast. Allied aircraft were warned to stay higher up or risk getting shot at. Behind the guns was a long single line of balloons, each trailing cables to enmesh and bring down a V1. Behind the balloons were patrols of fighters.

The fighters circled at about 8,000 ft. The pilots scanned the area below them for the tell-tale flame of the ramjet. Once a V1 was spotted, the pilot would dive down to gain speed and get behind the V1. It proved difficult to hit such a small target at about 400 yards, but if fire was opened at under 200 yards the fighter risked being engulfed by the resulting

A V1 which came down near Ashford in July 1944 is inspected by a salvage team.

explosion. Even more dangerous was for the fighter to fly alongside the V1 and use its wingtip to give the flying bomb a nudge. This upset the gyroscope guidance system and caused it to drop out of the sky. Unfortunately, the V1 could explode as it was nudged, so the feat was discouraged by Hill.

In the first month of the V1 assault, the Germans launched 4,361 weapons, of which about 1,000 malfunctioned, 300 were brought down by guns or balloons and 924 were shot down by fighters. That left about 2,000 that got through to bring random death and destruction to towns and villages across southern England.

Seen from an RAF aircraft, the sky over the south coast is filled with barrage balloons positioned at the correct height and location to stand a good chance of bringing down a V1.

*An anti-aircraft gun crew blast the skies over the south coast as
a V1 comes in off the sea.*

On 8 September, a huge explosion in Chiswick heralded the arrival of the V2. This was a very different weapon. It was a twelve ton rocket missile that carried a warhead of 1,650 lb. Instead of flying like a conventional aircraft, it was launched almost vertically to reach a height of about 50

A V2 rocket takes off. The V2 flew so high and fast that the Allies had no effective defence against it. It was said in London that you could tell the difference between a V1 and V2 because while the former demolished a house, the latter demolished a street.

miles before dropping down to its target at a speed of 2,000 mph. It was immune to guns, balloons or cables. There was nothing Hill and his pilots could do about the V2. The only answer was to defeat Germany.

The sheer scale of the V1 and V2 attacks caused great concern and worry among the civilian population, as Hitler had intended, but produced no desire for peace without victory. By October the main launch sites had been captured by advancing Allied armies in France and the V1 assaults slowed, though they did not end until February 1945.

By that date Fighter Command had a powerful new weapon in its armoury: the jet fighter Meteor. This aircraft was rushed into service at the end of July 1944 with 616 Squadron at Manston, specifically to meet the V1 threat. It proved to be highly effective in the new role.

A V1 launch ramp near Calais, photographed after its capture by advancing British troops in August 1944.

De Havilland Mosquito – Fighter

Type: Twin engined, two seat fighter
Engine: 2 x 1460 hp Rolls Royce Merlin 23
Wingspan: 54 ft 2 in
Length: 41 ft 9 in
Height: 15 ft 3 in
Weight: Empty 14,300 lb
Loaded 20,000 lb
Armament: 4 x 20 mm cannon in nose plus 4 x .303 in machine guns
Max speed: 407 mph
Ceiling: 39,000 ft
Range: 1770 miles (with drop tanks)
Production: 1579

The Mosquito was originally conceived as a fast bomber, but its superlative performance meant that even before the bomber version entered production a fighter version was being developed. It entered service early in 1942, but a lack of numbers meant that it had little impact on air combat until 1943. The formidable punch of the nose-mounted armament and its great speed made this a highly effective fighter. In March 1943 a radar-equipped night-fighter version began to be produced. The machine guns were taken out to make space for the radar, but the remaining four cannon proved perfectly adequate. Various models of the night-fighter were built, with different radars producing a variety of nose shapes for this aircraft. It remained in active service until 1950.

In October 1944 Fighter Command was re-established, as ADGB was merged with some units from the 2nd TAF – the remainder of the 2nd TAF being moved to bases on the continent to continue the war from there.

While the V-weapon attacks took place the more conventional German air attacks continued, although they became very much rarer. On 4 March 1945 came the last major raid. A total of more than 100 German night-fighters and bombers attacked British bomber bases just as RAF bombers

Gloster Meteor

Type:	Jet fighter
Engine:	2 x 1700 lb thrust
	Rolls-Royce Welland turbojets
Wingspan:	43 ft
Length:	41 ft 3 in
Height:	13 ft
Weight:	Empty 8140 lb
	Loaded 13,800 lb
Armament:	4 x 20 mm cannon
Max speed:	415 mph
Ceiling:	44,000 ft
Range:	1340 miles
Production:	230 (plus 3750 postwar)

The Messerschmitt Me262 jet fighter beat the Meteor into active service by just three weeks, but the Meteor remains the first Allied jet aircraft in combat. The first prototype flew in March 1943, but the development of the aircraft was dogged by continual engine problems and even when it entered service it was prone to breakdown with monotonous frequency. As the V1 offensive tailed off the one squadron equipped with Meteors was moved to the continent. Despite seeking combat, Meteor pilots never met the Me262; so no jet vs jet combats took place. After the war the Meteor became the standard RAF fighter, seeing service worldwide.

were returning from their night's work over the Reich. Great damage was done and 30 RAF bombers were destroyed. Although Kent was not attacked, its night-fighters were heavily employed once it was realised what was happening.

On 17 March a force of eighteen Junkers Ju88 bombers left bases in the Netherlands to bomb England; little damage was done. It was the last time enemy aircraft flew over Britain. Fighter Command's job was done.

It had been a tough job, but a necessary one. In all, 3,690 aircrew from Fighter Command had been killed, 1,215 seriously wounded and 601 captured. They had shot down 5,000 enemy aircraft, and damaged many more. Fighter Command achieved much between 1939 and 1945, but nothing greater than the fact that they did not relinquish control of the air to the mighty Luftwaffe during those few fateful weeks in the late summer of 1940.

Today we look back on the Second World War as a victory for Britain and for democracy. Many of us lost family members. The pain of such loss fades with the years and for many younger people who were not alive then the missing uncle or grandfather is no more than a face in a faded photograph. But if Fighter Command had failed we would be looking back not only on defeat, but on years of life under the jackbooted heel of one of the most oppressive regimes ever to exist. As Churchill himself said, 'Never in the field of human conflict was so much owed by so many to so few.'

These men were heroes indeed.

Squadrons